MW00679199

UBS Monograph Series, No. 8

Anthropological Approaches to the Interpretation of the Bible

Krijn van der Jagt

UNITED BIBLE SOCIETIES
New York

United Bible Societies
Monograph Series

Contents

© 2002 by the United Bible Societies

All Rights Reserved

No part of this book may be translated or reproduced in any form without the written permission of the United Bible Societies.

Books in the series of **UBS Monographs** may be ordered from a national Bible Society or from either of the following centers:

UBS Europe Distribution Centre   American Bible Society
Danish Bible Society   1865 Broadway
Frederiksborggade 50   New York, NY 10023
DK 1360 Copenhagen K   U. S. A.
Denmark

L. C. Cataloging-in-Publication Data

Jagt, Krijn Adriaan van der, 1945-
    Anthropological approaches to the interpretation of the Bible / Krijn van der Jagt.
        p.   cm. – (UBS monograph series ; 8)
    Includes bibliographical references.
    ISBN 0-8267-0458-1
    1. Bible–Hermeneutics. 2. Christianity and Culture. 3. Anthropology. I. Title. II. Series.

BS476 .J295 2002
220.6'7–dc21

                                                2002028716
                                                CIP

UBS Monograph #8
Printed in the United States of America
ABS -7/03-250-QD2-112794

Foreword

This book grew out of four lectures I presented to the Triennial Workshop on Translation of the United Bible Societies, held in May 1997 in Merida, Mexico. In the lectures I introduced a number of anthropological approaches to the interpretation of the Bible.

I am grateful to Dr. Basil Rebera, the former Translation Services Coordinator of the United Bible Societies, who encouraged and supported me to do research in this particular area of Biblical studies.

My colleagues Dr. Robert Bascom and Dr. Lénart de Regt read large parts of the text of the book and offered me valuable comments. I am thankful for their contributions.

Drs. Philip Noss, Anthony Abela, and Michael Seleznev read parts of the draft. I thank them for their advice. Manuella van der Jagt advised me on the use of the English language. I thank her for her patience and good work.

The book introduces the reader to the application of Social Science in the area of Biblical Studies. This particular research is important for Bible translation. The book is written with the translator of the Bible in mind. It attempts to help Bible translators to bridge the gap between the cultures of the Ancient Near East and the cultures of the receptor languages. The main focus of the book is on culture and interpretation. The Bible is viewed as a cultural document, a collection of narratives of ancient communities, which can only be understood in the cultural context of the Ancient Near East.

All Biblical quotations in this book come from the New Revised Standard Version (NRSV), unless noted otherwise.

CONTENTS

Hebrew Transliteration Table

The following system of transliteration has been adopted in order to keep all references as simple as possible for those readers who are not trained in Hebrew.

The English vowels, *a, e, i, o,* and *u,* represent the nearest equivalent sounds of the corresponding Hebrew vowels. Gemination of consonants caused by *dagesh forte* is normally represented by the doubling of the printed consonant, but may also for simplicity be represented by a single consonant, according to the author's purpose. The presence of *dagesh lene* will not be reflected in the representation of *gimel, daleth,* and *kaf,* since the resulting difference in English pronunciation is negligible or nonexistent. Consonants are represented as follows:

א	'	ט	t	פ, ף	f
ב	b	י	y	צ, ץ	ts
ב	v	ק, ך	k	ק	q
ג	g	ל	l	ר	r
ד	d	מ, ם	m	שׂ	s
ה	h	נ, ן	n	שׁ	sh
ו	w	ס	s	ת	t
ז	z	ע	'	ת	th
ח	ch	פ	p		

Those who work with the Hebrew text will, of course, wish to consult their copies of the text directly.

Abbreviations Used in This Volume

General Abbreviations

A.D. *Anno Domini* (in the year
       of our Lord)
B.C.   Before Christ

NRSV   New Revised Standard
       Version

Books of the Bible

Gen	Genesis	Isa	Isaiah
Exo	Exodus	Jer	Jeremiah
Lev	Leviticus	Hos	Hosea
Num	Numbers	Matt	Matthew
Deut	Deuteronomy	2 Cor	2 Corinthians
Josh	Joshua	Php	Philippians
1,2 Sam	1,2 Samuel	Col	Colossians
2 Kgs	2 Kings	1 Thes	1 Thessalonians
Psa	Psalms		

Greek Transliteration Table

The following simplified system of transliteration for Greek has been followed so that those unacquainted with Greek will be able to understand the discussion.

α	a	ι	i	ρ	r
β	b	κ	k	σ, ς	s
γ	g	λ	l	τ	t
δ	d	μ	m	υ	u
ε	e	ν	n	φ	f
ζ	z	ξ	x	χ	ch
η	ei	ο	o	ψ	ps
θ	th	π	p	ω	ō

Introduction

The general aim of this book is to introduce anthropological approaches to the interpretation of the Bible. The Bible is a collection of books that can be studied from several angles. As the Holy Scripture of Jewish and Christian believers it is received as revelation of God and as a source of faith. The Biblical writings are also read from a different perspective, namely, as historical and cultural documents. An anthropological approach to the Bible focuses on the cultural world of the ancient texts.

The main objective of this book is to sketch the cultural world of the Ancient Near East as the wider context of the Bible. By the Ancient Near East, I mean the areas of the modern countries of Iran, Iraq, Turkey, Syria, Lebanon, Israel, Jordan, and Egypt.

An anthropological reading of the Bible exposes aspects of the text that remain more or less concealed in other types of reading; it has its own focus and areas of special interest. It sheds light on specific issues that other readings do not emphasize. It approaches an ancient Biblical text from typically anthropological angles. We can discern at least three main perspectives:

1. The sociological perspective views the ancient text as a collection of literary traditions of ancient communities. The Hebrew Bible contains traditions of ancient Israel and the New Testament presents us with ancient traditions of Christian communities in the Mediterranean region. The authors of the ancient texts lived in societies that were quite different from modern societies. A basic knowledge of the social context of the Bible is prerequisite for a meaningful interpretation of Biblical texts.
2. The historical perspective situates the Bible in a broad historical setting. The Bible is an important witness of the cultural evolution of humanity. The Biblical text reflects the growing consciousness of the human being in history as it highlights crucial breakthroughs in awareness and understanding. Anthropologists are particularly interested in the earliest strata of an ancient text. Their approach to ancient texts often resembles the methods used in archaeology.

   The historical approach focuses on the world-view of the ancient communities that produced Biblical texts. A reconstruction of Ancient Near Eastern religion constitutes a powerful model for the interpretation of the Bible.

1

3. The literary perspective takes full account of the nature of the text as literature. The ancient authors created texts and these were not merely pictures of a real world that existed in ancient times, but rather, literary creations, symbolic worlds. The Bible contains a set of narratives of communities. In the book of Genesis we find the narrative of the household of Abraham. This narrative became the charter of the monarchic state of David and Solomon. Later narratives reinterpreted this narrative in the light of new historical developments. The interpretation of narratives is a fundamental exercise in the anthropological approach of the Bible.

Culture and Anthropology

An anthropological approach to the Bible relates to the culture of the society that has produced the ancient texts. Anthropologists treat the Biblical text as a cultural system. Scholars who study an ancient Biblical text find themselves interpreting a cultural system that is quite distant from their own culture. In actuality, their work is very similar to Western anthropologists studying a foreign culture. The main difference is that the Biblical scholar cannot study the society that has produced the Biblical text directly. He or she has to work with texts only since the ancient society that produced the texts no longer exists as a living entity.

When the term anthropology is employed, cultural anthropology is implied. As the word itself shows, the object of research in anthropology is man. Cultural anthropology seeks to understand the human being as a cultural being. This means it views the human being as an *animal symbolicum*, a being whose nature it is to use elaborate systems of symbols in everyday life. The analysis of the systems of symbols should always lead to an understanding of the human being and not be limited to a mere understanding of systems. Following this train of thought, we can say that the study of the Biblical text-world, which is a system of symbols, should provide us with understanding of the human being.

Biblical scholars interpreting an ancient Biblical text are dealing with ancient culture. Thus they study a product of ancient thought. In this book I will indicate how and where anthropological methods and theories can help Biblical scholars to understand ancient thought as expressed in the Biblical text.

Culture and Cultural Systems

Culture is a very wide concept and it may refer to all human activity. It often contrasts with another wide concept, which is the concept of nature. In any situation where nature is being transformed by the human being, culture can be said to be in effect. The human being is a cultural being, and consequently he constantly transforms his environment.

The anthropologist, Clifford Geertz, views culture primarily as a system of symbols. This sounds like a rather abstract representation, but we should realize that culture is such a generic concept and we simply need to find some useful way of referring to it. Geertz's approach to culture focuses on the underlying patterns of all human activity, which he calls the symbolic. The human being as a cultural being does not live in a natural world but in a symbolic world. In this light we can say that the culture of a particular community comprises the totality of all symbolic forms available in that community. People resort to the symbolic structures of their community to reflect and to communicate. As mentioned before, culture is a very wide concept. Also, the statement that culture is a system of symbols tends to be too unspecific for practical use. Geertz therefore distinguishes between several cultural systems within a particular culture. These systems are language, art, myth, ritual, theory, theology, philosophy, politics, architecture, and many others. These cultural systems have a varying degree of coherence and relate to other systems within the total culture in multiple ways. In addition, the general system, the culture of a given community as a whole, knows a certain degree of coherence.

Symbols and Meaning

Culture is always concerned with symbols and meaning. The human being uses symbolic structures to express his experience of life. Life experience is characterized by variety and vicissitude. It is experienced not only as a struggle for survival often exposed as a shortage of essential goods, but also as a spiritual adventure. Human beings are always in search of meaning as this is part of their very nature.

Human beings have a strong urge to express their experience and need symbolic systems to do so. Symbols therefore function as vehicles for hopes, beliefs, and values. Apart from expressing significance, human beings also use symbolic structures as a tool to control behavior. The cultural systems in use in a given community provide for control mechanisms, recipes or programs, similar to computer programs, which regulate the brain to induce culturally, accepted behavior. Humans cannot live by instincts alone, they need culture and depend on symbolic systems that guide their behavior.

Humans cannot live without knowledge of the world they live in. They develop models of reality, which serve to describe and understand the world around them and guide their perception. Models are specific symbolic structures. In the first chapter of Genesis, a model of the world is given that served to aid the ancient peoples in the understanding of their environment. The representation of the sky as the roof of the world having an attic with stores for hail and snow was instrumental for the explanation of the natural phenomena of hail and snow.

In the Bible anthropologists find a variety of symbolic forms that have served in the ancient communities as means of expression, tools for controlling, and models of reality. The Bible as a whole can be viewed as a collection of interconnected symbolic systems.

Animal Symbolicum

Man is indeed an *animal symbolicum*, as he exists in a symbolic universe. This universe comprises all symbolic systems that are in use in the community he lives in. The human being can only know and be known within and through his symbolic universe. An anthropological approach to the Bible therefore aims at an understanding of the symbolic universe of the ancient writers of the Biblical texts. It attempts to bridge the gap between the ancient writer and modern man.

Chapter 1

Anthropological Approaches of Ancient Texts

Problems with Interpretation

The interpretation of cultural systems largely depends on the analysis of the meaning of symbols. The same applies to the interpretation of a text. A text is a specific symbolic structure, a unit of meaning that is part of a larger web of symbolic representation. A particular text of the Hebrew Bible, be it a poem, a narrative or a legal text, relates to a number of cultural systems. These systems are part of the overall cultural system we call the culture of ancient Israel. Thus a given text cannot be interpreted in isolation.

When we are studying a particular text from the Hebrew Bible, we must be able to position that text within the overall cultural system of ancient Israel. We have to relate that text to all relevant cultural systems, such as language, narrative art, poetry, social structure, family religion, Yahwistic theology, and others.

A sound interpretation of a text depends on a number of things. Firstly, it depends on how well the language the text has been written in has been understood. Secondly, it depends on to what extent the meaning of specific key concepts has been grasped. Thirdly, it depends on whether specific structures within the text have been understood, such as specific rhetoric structures and specific models that have been used to refer to reality. Generally speaking, this means how adequately the text has been related to all relevant cultural systems and how well these systems have been understood. While studying a Biblical text, we may find ourselves in "a forest of symbols," to borrow a phrase from the anthropologist Victor Turner (1967). The interpreter of a given text needs to discover the meaning of a great variety of symbols and symbolic structures.

Biblical texts often refer to non-verbal symbols such as blood, water, and fat, as well as specific actions such as taking one's shoe off and casting it on the ground. Scholars of a Biblical text are expected to deal with meanings embedded in a variety of symbolic forms. They have to analyze models, metaphors, and literary motifs, and finally, they must unearth the basic values underlying the message of the text. It is important to keep in mind that the interpretation of culture, and consequently, the interpretation of text, can never be regarded as being fully completed. Thus it can be said

5

that interpretation of text is intrinsically incomplete. I would like to focus on four prominent constituents of Biblical text that are often crucial for a meaningful interpretation, namely: description, concept, metaphor and narrative.

Description

An anthropologist who studies cultural systems in a fieldwork situation will reach a point where he has to record his findings. He must describe the cultural system he researches. When describing culture, we are bound to the use of language, which, in turn, can be considered a rather inadequate tool, as it tends to work in a linear manner. Culture has many facets or dimensions and language can prove to be very limited in its expression of culture. Anthropologists often describe foreign cultures in a language that is not part of the cultural system they research. This complicates the work even further as the foreign language does not harbor the tailored instruments to describe the culture efficiently.

Geertz has made a famous distinction with respect to description of culture. He refers to a distinction between "thick" and "thin" descriptions (2000:3-30). A "thin" description is factual; it is an objective one in which anthropologists describe what they see and hear. "Thin" types of description do not reveal the meaning behind words and do not hint at what particular behavior expresses, while "thick" ones do.

Human behavior is cultural and therefore symbolic. If an anthropologist would have to describe the village life of a particular ethnic group, he would not reveal much by simply stating the facts. For instance, if he only reports what he sees by summing up where the houses and fields are located, he does not reveal anything of interest to those who concern themselves with the interpretation of culture. To them the fascination lies beyond the facts where the pattern of thought of the people is revealed; thus the facts are uninteresting. The fact that the people from a particular ethnic group always leave their village in the direction of the east cannot be explained by another fact, namely that the only outgoing roads can be found on the east side of the village. The people who need to go to the fields situated on the west side of the village have to leave the village from the east side and then make a sharp turn backwards. However, the thoughts that lie behind the facts are significant and it is the anthropologist's responsibility to reveal the thoughts behind the facts. Leaving the village in a westerly direction is believed to cause harm to the village. This thought is culturally significant and the anthropologist should convey this to his reader. Thus meaningful description of culture needs to be "thick" description.

I feel that the distinction Geertz makes between "thick" and "thin" types of description facilitates the understanding of the specific nature of description we find in the ancient Biblical texts. In that situation we do not read descriptions of anthropologists who refer to a foreign culture, but we have descriptions of ancient Israelite people, who describe their own culture in their own language. It is important to understand that it is the

indigenous point of view that is presented in the Biblical accounts. The reader of a Biblical text must therefore make an attempt to discover the indigenous perspective of the ancient text.

The ancient historiography we find in the Hebrew Bible is dominated by "thick" description. The historical events described in the books of 1-2 Kings, for instance, are not meant to be factual but are primarily theological in nature. The author did not want to present an objective account of the merits of each king; rather he indicated whether or not each individual king had tolerated cultic activity at the sacrificial places (Hebrew *bamoth*) in the countryside.

As modern historiography tends to aim at completeness and objectivity, ancient historiography is different. It does not focus on facts as much. Instead, it expresses thoughts and beliefs. This does not imply that ancient historiography produces false accounts of the past; it presents colored pictures, which should be interpreted in the light of particular theological values. For example, a Biblical author may not want to give a factual description of a city gate in a particular context. A gate of a city is often treated as a cultural symbol in Biblical texts and not just as a building. References to the gate and its dimensions are aimed at expressing emotions and values, such as protection and security.

When the Biblical author describes the ark of Noah, and he presents the dimensions of that life saving boat, obviously his intent is not to remain objective in his account. Thus his description is a "thick" one. If a translator of the Bible does not recognize this, and opts for a very factual and exact rendering of these dimensions, he may not convey the intended meaning. A modern person reading the Bible easily misreads descriptions in the ancient text and interprets "thick" descriptions as "thin." This has been a common error in interpretation and translation.

Description and Prescription

In the Bible there is also a considerable amount of prescriptive language. The law texts in the Pentateuch are prescriptive in nature. Again, we should be aware of the particular character of prescriptive language since prescription can be considered to be "thick." This means that the prescription does not necessarily reflect historical facts about actual law and custom, instead, the world-view of the writers is presented. The legal texts reveal the order of the world as perceived by the community and indicate how people should have behaved. It is not always certain whether a particular law or rule we find in the Bible actually had been practiced in ancient Israel.

Concepts

I have previously endeavored to elicit some aspects of the relationship between language and culture. We saw that language is a very particular

cultural system among those of a culture, as it mirrors all other systems. In every culture specific concepts are developed and these concepts relate to the perception of life of the community. All cultures develop concepts concerning the self and others, nature, work, time, power, sickness, and the supernatural. If one desires to understand the thoughts of a group of people, one should attempt to analyze the manner in which those people have conceptualized. In every culture people tend to have set ideas about what a human being really is, what humans should aspire to be, and in which manner they should behave.

Geertz provides a very interesting example of a culture in Java, Indonesia (1983:59-62). In Javanese culture two terms are used to refer to the human being, to the self. The self is perceived to consist of two parts: the inner and outer part. The inner world is perceived as being refined and pure as opposed to the outer world, which is rough. Ideally, man must keep his inner world pure and calm. Also, he must maintain a sense of inner peace and have smooth relations with the outside world despite his rough exterior. He does this by means of politeness. The Javanese concepts expressing these qualities are referred to by Geertz as "local terms" or "experience-near concepts" (1983:57). In anthropological literature, also the terms "emic" and "etic" are used in this respect. "Emic" terms are the same as what Geertz calls "experience-near concepts" or "local terms." These are culture specific, in contrast to "etic" terms, which belong to the universal jargon of modern science and global culture.

Every culture has developed a concept of the self. This was also the case in ancient Israel. The Hebrew concept of *nephesh* expresses the Israelite cultural perception of the self. This concept refers to a particular conception of the human being that was new in the cultural world of the Ancient Near East: the human as an independent person. In ancient Israelite culture, the human being was seen as a striving and struggling being. The human being was perceived as a "living soul," a being that had the principle of life in him. The concept contains the idea of an independent being that is primarily responsible for his life. In ancient Israel man was no longer perceived as an object, a toy of the gods, a thought that was widely held in the Ancient Near East.

Nephesh is a "local concept" in Geertz's terminology. There are many instances of these "local concepts" in the Hebrew Bible. It is crucial for any translation of the Hebrew Bible to translate these concepts contextually, as these terms are charged with meaning.

Metaphors

The invention of metaphor in language can be compared to that of the wheel in technology. In a metaphoric expression, an image of something that is known is used to refer to something that is not known. When a person attempts to speak about the unknown and all that lies beyond his perception, he frequently makes use of metaphors. Metaphors can function as instruments that are used to create a world beyond the empirical world.

Ancient religious texts are rich in metaphoric expressions. One can say that these texts are real networks of metaphors. Metaphors are special symbols or signs that carry the core of the message the writer intends to communicate. They reflect the perception and cognition of specific cultures.

In Biblical texts we find a variety of metaphors that refer to the ultimate, which is God. Metaphors of God, as a parent, a father or mother, a warrior, a shepherd, a rock and so on, express ancient thoughts concerning the divine. "The LORD is my rock" (Psa 18.2) is a metaphor that expresses the relationship of the faithful with the divine, as well as particular qualities ascribed to the divine. Metaphors are windows that can shed light on the religious thought of the people who wrote the ancient texts. Both concepts and metaphors are key elements of Biblical texts. They need special analytical care in the art of interpretation.

Narrative

We encounter a great deal of narration in the Hebrew Bible. The Biblical narratives are not only fine pieces of art and entertaining for reading but also serve as sources that facilitate the understanding of the culture of ancient Israel. Narration is, in actuality, a powerful way of expressing how the world is perceived. Just as description, concept, and metaphor reveal specific cultural meaning, narrative is a window on culture. The narrator reveals important points of view, specific knowledge, and culturally important values by using his own voice and by using the characters of his narrative.

The Hebrew Bible is an extremely varied piece of work; it consists of texts featuring legends, etiological narratives, mythological and biographical narratives, folktales, and other genres. In all these texts we come across narrative. Narrative, just as description, is an ingredient that is found in a great variety of text types. We also find narrative where the modern person would not expect it, for example, in legal texts and historiographical texts. Narration is a basic tool in ancient writings; it is used to express culture in a wider sense of the word.

A good number of Biblical narratives are quests. In such narratives the hero of the story embarks on a journey to search for something of great value. During the journey the hero encounters many difficulties, but in the end he reaches his destiny. The itinerary narratives of the patriarchs in the book of Genesis, as well as the narratives of the wanderings of Moses and the Israelites in the deserts, all reflect aspects of the quest story.

The narrator of a story communicates important values to his hearer or reader. He uses the plot of the story as well as the dialogues of the characters as mediums of expression. The most powerful voice is often the narrator himself. The narrators of the Hebrew Bible are omniscient. They are in a position to reveal what is hidden in the hearts of men and even in the heart of God. The narrator has an overview of history; he knows why things happen as they happen and what the ultimate truth is behind the

events of a story. Narrative analysis is therefore an extremely important discipline in an anthropological approach to the Biblical text.

The Larger Narratives in the Bible

The Bible contains a number of larger narratives. When using the term narrative in this perspective, the term is used in a broader sense. It takes the function of theology and ideology. The narrative of the Exodus out of Egypt, for instance, inspired all the clans and tribes of Israel. It created identity and provided destiny for the people of Israel throughout the centuries. The message of the narrative is that Yahweh, the God of Israel, was able to overcome the powerful gods of Egypt and to liberate his people from slavery. The obvious assumption is the following: no one can challenge this God, his power surpasses all powers. The Exodus theology became a major constituent of Israelite religious thought.

In the Davidic-Solomonic period a very powerful narrative was created. It was the narrative of the blessing of the household of Abraham. The time of David and Solomon was a period of unequaled expansion for Israel. All the tribes of Israel were united under a king from the tribe of Judah and many neighboring tribes were made vassals. Numerous smaller ethnic communities were incorporated into the reign of David. Abraham had indeed become a father of many nations and in him many peoples received the blessing of peace and prosperity (Gen 12).

The narrative of the family of Abraham created identity, provided legitimacy for the political status quo of the day, and became a foundational narrative for the royal house of David (Gen 49.8-12). The building stones of this narrative are ancestor legends, which existed in oral form before they were incorporated in a written text (van der Jagt 1994).

The core of the larger narrative of the book of Genesis (Gen 12–50) was enlarged in later periods of Israel's history with the narrative of David (1 Sam 16–2 Sam 24) and the narrative of Jerusalem (Isa 2). After the monarchic period, the entire narrative was reinterpreted in the light of Messianic beliefs (Isa 11).

Another powerful narrative was the one of the holy and pure people governed by a holy and pure high priest. This narrative was established in the post-exilic period when the Judean community was directed by the priestly class. The core of this narrative we find in the book of Leviticus. The writer of the Epistle to the Hebrews takes up this narrative and reinterprets it in the light of the belief in the risen Christ. In his perspective the people of God, the believers in Christ, are a purified nation, cleansed by the blood of the pure and faithful high priest Jesus Christ.

Victor H. Matthews and Don C. Benjamin (1993) suggest that the four sources of the Pentateuch, which are the Elohist, the Yahwist, the Deuteronomist, and the Priestly source, go back to four larger narratives. The Elohist is the foundational narrative of a northern state before the Davidic state, the Yahwist is the foundational narrative of the Davidic state,

10

the Deuteronomist is the foundational narrative of the state of Judah, and the Priestly is the foundational narrative of Judaism as a distinct religion.

All larger narratives in the Bible are interconnected. Biblical texts echo other Biblical texts; allusion and quotation play an important role in Biblical literature. Intertextuality is a major feature in the entire Bible. This is very obvious when we carefully look at the major narratives of the New Testament. One of the powerful narratives of Jesus of Nazareth has influenced the minds of millions over centuries: the poor and the meek will inherit the earth. The message of this narrative however resounds the voices of Israel's prophets. The words of Jesus are both fulfilment and application of the prophetic words of the Old Testament. The narrative of Paul of Tarsus has inspired Christian religion profoundly: Jesus is risen from the dead, he has conquered death, and all who are united with him in spirit will also conquer death. It's message resounds Israel's belief in a God who can conquer all powers, even the invincible powers of the Egyptian kings. So the Exodus narrative and the resurrection narrative are interconnected.

A meaningful interpretation of the larger Biblical narratives in the cultural context of the Ancient Near East is the key to all interpretation of Biblical text. Translating the Bible is often characterized as translating the message of the Bible. Translators therefore should identify the messages of all larger narratives in order to understand the intertextuality of the Scriptures.

An Anthropological Approach

An anthropological approach to Biblical studies cannot be considered to be an entirely new method of research. In fact, it can be viewed as broadening the historical-critical method. The emphasis on the quest for the *Sitz im Leben* of the ancient text is a similar approach. The historical-critical method receives a more refined set of instruments from an anthropological approach. These instruments come from social science and linguistics. An anthropological approach situates the text in the cultural context of the Ancient Near East. The *Sitz im Leben* is to be defined in terms of culture; context in the anthropological perspective is cultural context.

An anthropological approach promotes the application of methods used in social sciences. However, the use of anthropological and sociological instruments to interpret ancient text is hampered due to the incompleteness of the data concerning the Ancient Near Eastern cultures. Ancient Biblical texts are often incomplete in their description of rituals and customs. Scholars frequently encounter allusions to ancient customs when studying the texts. Often they do not find full descriptions and are thus forced to reconstruct meaning relying on an inadequate set of data. A great number of texts in the Hebrew Bible remain somewhat obscure since we do not have sufficient knowledge of the cultural context. We lack specific information about the religious customs of the ancient world and this is a major setback in our scholarly pursuit of the Bible.

Anthropologists have managed to collect a vast amount of data on religion and ritual from across the various cultures of the world over the years. The religious culture of the Near East has changed considerably over the centuries under the influence of the great monotheistic religions. In other parts of the world, traditional religions have remained practically unchanged until recent times. Certain rituals that were known and practiced in the ancient world are still known in other parts of the world. Anthropology can thus shed light on obscure Biblical texts from the understanding of religion and ritual obtained through research on contemporary cultures of Asia and Africa. We should not forget that human culture is universal and that people are psychologically equal. Although cultures differ in many respects, there are remarkable cross-cultural parallels. People are cultural beings, so the people of the Ancient Near East are not exceptional. The challenges of life and the potential to face the challenges are basically common to all people. The cultures of the Ancient Near East fit in the evolution of human culture. The modes of thought of the ancient peoples are intelligible for us, modern people, as well as their languages and cultures, although we need to make special efforts to bridge the gaps history has created.

Reading Scenarios

In an anthropological approach, a Biblical text is seen as part of culture. The text is a unit of meaning in which different cultural systems function. It is therefore not possible to use a linear, one-dimensional method of interpretation. The very nature of the text requires a multi-dimensional approach. A multi-dimensional approach to the interpretation of Biblical text can be obtained by using different reading scenarios. A reading scenario functions as a lens. One looks at the text through a lens and by doing so one zooms in on one of the cultural systems that feature in the text (Neyrey 1991:3-25). When one looks at a text through a particular lens, certain aspects of meaning surface, and by focusing on particular points, the reader gains insight into the entire unit. Consequently, it is crucial to know where to focus. In a given text, a number of cultural systems dominate the entire unit. Hence it is important to identify the cultural systems that are dominant. Zooming in on those systems will lead to a meaningful interpretation of the text. I would like to demonstrate this with a text from the Hebrew Bible, the book of Job. I will try out three different reading scenarios. First, I will read the text as a narrative; second, the text will be approached from the point of view of social values, and third, from the perspective of ritual. These three scenarios complement one another and all three are needed for finding the most meaningful interpretation of the text.

Chapter 2

An Anthropological Approach
to the Book of Job

Genre

The book of Job is an ancient narrative that has features of both legend and myth. Many of the narratives in the Hebrew Bible are recounted legends. The heroes of the Biblical narratives are famous men and women from the past. They were very courageous, pious, and faithful. Their lives were eventful and fruitful in a very special way. The narratives about the patriarchs and matriarchs, the judges, and some of the prophets fall in this category. Most of these legendary narratives harbor mythic elements as well. In a mythic narrative we encounter supernatural beings as characters. These beings play specific roles in the plot of the narrative. Sons of God, members of the celestial court, play a major role in the prelude of the flood narrative (Gen 6). A special character, who is called the angel of the LORD, occurs frequently throughout the Hebrew Bible. Spirits and demons also appear in the Biblical stories.

God himself is often introduced in a Biblical narrative as a main character and a partner of the hero of the story. God often appears to the hero of a narrative in a mysterious way and enters in a dialogue with him, such as in many of the Abraham narratives.

In a legend the main characters are legendary ancestors while in a myth supernatural beings dominate. In the book of Job we meet both human beings and supernatural beings as characters of the plot. Job and his friends are the human characters, and the Creator and Satan are the supernatural characters. The narrative of Job is best characterized as a recounted legend with mythic elements.

The book has prose and poetic parts. The prose parts contain the main plot of the story. The plot is embellished with lengthy dialogues written in a poetic style. These have didactic aspects and present themes of the ancient Israelite wisdom. The poetic and narrative parts form a single literary unit. We cannot cut the book into separate semi-independent parts, as it is a whole and should be interpreted as such.

Narrative as Reading Scenario

The first reading scenario we employ is the narrative model. We read the whole book as one narrative. It is the narrative of Job, a legendary rich man from the land of Uz. The hero is not only rich; he is also presented as a very pious and righteous man. He is the embodiment of the perfect man, a true legend.

The narrative has a simple plot: the hero of the story suddenly encounters great suffering; he loses everything he has, including his health, in a single day. Job is the object of a contest between God and Satan, the public prosecutor at the heavenly court. God and Satan contest whether Job is indeed perfect, or whether he can be tempted to commit sin. Satan argues that Job will openly curse God as soon as he loses all he has acquired in life. Job is completely unaware of the contest. He cannot understand why God changed his fate from bliss to suffering overnight.

The middle part of the book contains lengthy dialogues between Job and his friends. His encounters with his friends are in fact bitter fights. Job's friends did not just come to console him; they turned out to be his adversaries instead of his friends. They try their utmost to bring Job down in order to make him accept that he is not the perfect man he presumes to be. They feel he should admit defeat and confess the evil he has committed. Job's dialogues with his friends are fierce contests about who and what is right. Job's friends offer the thesis that God, the judge of the whole world, does not punish innocent people. Job resists vehemently and insists on his complete innocence.

During the course of their dialogue, Job curses the day he was born. He wishes he was not born, and above all, he wants to see that justice is revealed. He challenges God to come forward and present his case. Job wants to meet God in person for a contest since he is convinced that God has to confirm in public that Job is righteous and has done no evil.

In the last part of the book, God reveals himself to Job in a storm. He answers Job in an indirect manner by describing himself as the definitive and crafty creator of the world. First, he points at the marvels of his wisdom, his extensive knowledge and skill as architect of the world, and his extraordinary power to control all the elements of nature, including the monsters of the sea. Job then is confronted with his own ignorance and limitations that contrast sharply with God's abilities.

This experience leads Job to basic insight (Hebrew *binah*) about God, life, and himself. Job understands that he cannot challenge God in any way, not even in the bizarre circumstances he finds himself in. Job accepts defeat in his contest with God in the following words from Job 42.5-6:

> I had heard of you by the hearing of the ear,
>   but now my eye sees you;
> therefore I despise myself,
>   and repent in dust and ashes.

The Quest of Job

The story of Job has the elements of a quest. His friends, who come to console him in his suffering, take the hero of the narrative on a philosophical journey. He embarks on an allegorical, long and difficult journey. Just as in a classical quest, the hero encounters great suffering, humiliation and anguish, yet he is persistent in his search for the treasure. The journey Job embarks on is a spiritual one, and the treasure he searches for is the value of wisdom. The hero finds the treasure at the end of the story; he finds the stone of wisdom when God, who is the only one who has access to wisdom, reveals himself to Job.

The Message of the Book of Job

The book of Job is written with a clear purpose, it is meant to impart wisdom to the reader. Hence wisdom is the most prominent value communicated through the message in the book. In the middle of the book, in chapter 28, we find a very important discourse, a poem on wisdom. Chapter 28 is indeed a key chapter in the book of Job. It tells the reader in beautiful poetic language that wisdom is out of reach for the human being and that only God has access to wisdom. In Job 28.12-13 we read:

> But where shall wisdom be found?
> And where is the place of understanding?
> Mortals do not know the way to it,
> and it is not found in the land of the living.

Only God has access to wisdom according to Job 28.23:

> God understands the way to it,
> and he knows its place.

Wisdom and God are almost equated and become interchangeable concepts in the book of Job. This is a very special feature of the book. The hero of the narrative finds wisdom in an encounter with the Creator. He humbles himself before the Creator of the world and this action transforms him from a foolish to a wise man. The underlying message of the story is that a human being needs to humble himself before God in order to find the treasure that is wisdom. The encounter with God is the climax of the whole story; it leads directly to a reversal of the situation. Job regains all he lost in a miraculous way. He is restored to his former status of being the richest man in the world and there the narrative ends.

In applying the reading scenario of the quest, the discourse as a whole becomes accessible. However, there are a few remaining problems for the reader and we need to rely on other scenarios to deal with these problems. For instance, how can it be explained that Job's friends, who came with good intentions to console him, ended up in bitter fights with the poor man? Why

is it that they deserved the severe punishment of death? It seems they had not done anything to deserve that fate and yet the narrator implies that the friends could not continue to live and must die. It appears that we need an additional reading scenario to make the text transparent in this respect.

Social Values in Ancient Narratives

When a modern person reads an ancient narrative, he or she has problems with the social values communicated through the plot of the story. The modern reader does not share all the values the narrator holds. There is often a clash of values between the narrator and the modern reader that hinders both appreciation and interpretation. A reader needs to be informed about the social values of the narrator as this helps the understanding of the social context in which the story is situated. The reader needs to look through the eyes of the narrator and grasp the value system he employed. The perception of social values has to function as a lens in this respect.

When we apply the core social values of Ancient Near Eastern societies to the book of Job, we can understand why the characters in the Job narrative behaved in the manner they did. We will now use social values as a reading scenario, which will lead to important insights into the Job narrative.

Social Values as Reading Scenario

To ensure our full understanding of the social setting of the narrative, we need to identify which social values dominated social life in the Ancient Near East. A group of scholars, Victor H. Matthews, Don C. Benjamin, and Claudia V. Camp (1996), have approached the cultural background of the Biblical text by using what they know of the basic value system of the contemporary Mediterranean world. They argue that Mediterranean culture has altered very little over the years and that the same basic values that were dominant in the Ancient Near East still determine the world-view of the present population. It is believed that models, taken from contemporary Mediterranean anthropology and sociology, can be applied to the Ancient Near Eastern text and yield results for meaningful interpretation.

The basic value system in Mediterranean society is the "honor-shame" complex. When reading the ancient texts, such as the books of 1-2 Samuel, it becomes apparent that honor and shame played a dominant role in the perception of life in ancient Israel. The society was based on honor. It applied to all people whose main drive in life was to avoid shame and to acquire honor. Ancient Near Eastern societies were antagonistic societies. At various levels, particularly among the elite, a fierce competition for honor tainted daily life. I will be dealing with the "honor-shame" complex in greater detail in Chapter 5. At this point I would like to apply the "honor-shame" complex as a reading scenario to the Job narrative without further explanation.

The Honor-Shame Complex

In honor-oriented societies, male members are continually in the act of challenging one another. These challenges can take the form of testing. For instance, one can test another's generosity, skills, or knowledge. As soon as one claims certain achievements in public, one can be challenged by another person. A challenge demands a riposte. If the riposte is successful, it brings honor to the person who was challenged and shame to the challenger who was unsuccessful in challenging his adversary.

In the book of Job, we come across a number of challenges and ripostes. Satan challenged God. He predicted that Job would curse God when he would lose his riches. Satan lost his challenge. Job never cursed God as Satan had predicted.

Job then challenged God. He wanted God to accept that he was an innocent man. He went very far in his challenge, but he did not curse the Creator. This means he did not shame God but continued to honor his Creator. Consequently, God was duly honored by his victory over Satan and the latter was utterly shamed by his defeat. Job lost his challenge to God; he accepted his defeat, humbled himself, and accepted the fact that he had put shame upon himself.

In addition to these challenges, Job's friends challenged him. They wanted to prove that Job was wrong in his assumption that he was innocent. They claimed to know the moral order of the world and what the cause of suffering was, but it turned out that they did not know. They did not speak what was right of God (43.7). Their error was not a light offense; it was an act of dishonoring God. They heaped shame on themselves, lost their honor, and the author implies in the text that they were bound to die. This type of death is called an "honor-killing" and is still in practice in different situations in contemporary honor-oriented societies.

A story such as the Job narrative cannot be interpreted outside of the honor-shame complex of Ancient Near Eastern societies. It is difficult for a modern person to imagine that God enters in an honor contest with Satan. It is even more difficult to understand that the righteous God brings great suffering on Job for the sole purpose of winning his contest with Satan. The story of Job can only maintain its meaning in the context of the imaginary world of a narrative situated in an honor-oriented society. We have seen that social values are a relevant reading scenario. We will now turn to another reading scenario, namely to ritual.

Ritual as Reading Scenario

Ritual and ritual thinking were important elements in the ancient world. Ancient man believed that the world was shaped by ritual performed in primordial times and that the reenacting of those ancient rituals in the present guaranteed the continuation of life. It was universally believed that changes in the status and role of a person, as well as all types of transformations of beings, could only be effectuated by performing the appropriate

17

ritual. This also applied to the crossing of boundaries in time and space. It was widely acknowledged that one could not change from a boy into a man or from a girl into a wife unless rituals were performed. Ancient society was held together by a wide variety of rituals.

In anthropological literature all rituals that are meant to induce changes in people, as well as those that effectuate crossings of boundaries in time and space, are categorized under the heading, "rites of passage." I will be dealing with these particular rituals in greater detail in Chapter 8. Ancient authors, as well the author of the book of Job, thought in terms of ritual. Therefore, it is valuable to search for patterns of ritual thought in the book of Job.

Ritual in the Book of Job

We encounter ritual both at the beginning of the narrative and at the end. Job is introduced to the reader in a context of ritual. At the beginning of the narrative, we find Job in the process of making a sacrifice on behalf of his children. Similarly, at the end of the narrative he prays to save the lives of his friends. Introducing a main character of a story in the context of ritual is conventional in Hebrew narrative. The book of 1 Samuel also begins with ritual. Also, the narrative of Gideon in the book of Judges opens with a ritual event. Gideon is introduced as the main character of the story while he is sacrificing.

The description of the ritual event is not just a part of the narrative; ritual has a special function in the discourse of the narrative. It is a structural component that carries specific meaning. In the story of Job, it is shown that Job changed during the course of the ordeal he underwent. All changes are effectuated by ritual in the ancient cultural context and this is also the underlying thought in the book of Job. We may expect ritual at turning points in the story and this is precisely what we find in the book of Job. At a crucial point towards the end of the narrative, Job's friends receive the following assignment:

> Now therefore take seven bulls and seven rams, and go to my servant Job, and offer up for yourselves a burnt offering; and my servant Job shall pray for you, for I will accept his prayer not to deal with you according to your folly; for you have not spoken of me what is right, as my servant Job has done (Job 42.8).

The narrative ends with a burnt sacrifice to expiate the sins of Job's friends and with a prayer of Job. The prayer is not just a request to God but an effective ritual. The hero of the narrative is transformed from an ordinary person into a prophet. This transformation is effectuated by appropriate ritual action. Job has undergone a change; he has become a prophet, a man of God, whose prayer is instrumental for saving the lives of his friends. Ritual thinking is a constitutive element in the entire discourse. The change in the life of Job is effectuated by ritual. The ordeal of his suffering has to

be interpreted as a ritual. Therefore, the whole narrative can be read as an account of a rite of passage.

The Book of Job as a Rite of Passage

I have suggested that we can read the book of Job as an account of a rite of passage. This suggestion may not be obvious at this point. It may be helpful, then, to give more background. When we closely examine the structure of the rite of passage, we notice that all rites of passage follow a similar pattern. There are always three stages in this ritual process:

1. The separation from the old situation.
2. The liminal period, which is the threshold period between the old and the new situation.
3. The aggregation, which is an integration into the new situation as a new person.

The narrative of Job suits the pattern of a rite of passage. Job has been separated from his social surroundings as a result of the loss of all his possessions and his health. During his liminal period, he is severely tested and even humiliated by his friends. His aggregation takes place by his vindication and installation as a prophet. I could elicit more features from the text to demonstrate the ritual aspects that are in the discourse. However, I would like to refer you to Chapter 8, which contains a detailed and more extensive coverage of the meaning of the symbols used in rites of passage.

Other Reading Scenarios, Key Concepts, and Models

In addition to the three reading scenarios that have been applied to the Job narrative, we could use other scenarios. For instance, we could focus on the social location of the implied author. Was the author a member of the rich elite? Did the author wish to communicate a message about the justification of wealth in a society where few happy, rich people lived together with masses of poor people? This may well have been the case. However, we do not know enough about the author and the intended audience.

Despite the fact that we only used three reading scenarios, the three have provided ample insight into the narrative. It is also important to make an analysis of the important concepts used in the text: wisdom (Hebrew *chokmah*), knowledge (Hebrew *da'at*), and planning (Hebrew *'etsah*). Also, special attention should be given to the specific metaphors that are employed. In particular, the metaphors for the divine are significant. The metaphors for Yahweh as the architect and judge exemplify this.

There is also an important model related to the cosmology of the book of Job. It requires special attention and can be regarded as a major constituent

of the narrative. According to its cosmology, God has created the world as a house founded on pillars and covered by a roof. The attic is a storage room for hail and snow. God himself is seated on the roof and watches over the limited space of the house beneath him.

Traditional Interpretations

Quite a few exegetes have tried to read the book of Job as an essay on theodicy, which is the defense of God's justice, goodness and power in view of the existence of evil. By doing this there is a danger of relating the narrative to a cultural system that is not part of the Ancient Near Eastern culture. A theodicy is a difficult issue within the context of a monotheistic and monistic world-view, but less problematic in the cultural world of the Ancient Near East. The book of Job poses the theodicy question, but it is not the main theme of the book and it does not answer it. An anthropological approach to the interpretation of the book of Job does lead to concrete results. It helps the reader to situate the text in its cultural context.

Chapter 3

Religion and Culture in the Ancient Near East

The most powerful reading scenario for the Bible is the religious system of the Ancient Near East. Religious values and concepts are dominant structures in the entire Bible. A large part of the Bible can be characterized as ancient religious text. It is therefore essential to present a brief analysis of the ancient religions of the Near East in general, and of the ancient religion of Israel in particular. Although religion did not exist as a separate domain in ancient cultures as it does in modern times, I will focus on the religious realm since the religious system functions as the backbone of the overall world-view. At this point I need to clarify the relationship between religion and culture, taking into account that this a fundamental issue in my discourse.

Religion as Cultural System

Religion is part of culture. It can be viewed as a specific symbolic structure within the overall system of a given culture. Geertz defines religion in the following way: "A system of symbols which acts to establish powerful, pervasive, and long lasting moods and motivations in men by formulating conceptions of a general order of existence and clothing these conceptions with such an aura of factuality that the moods and motivations seem uniquely realistic" (2000:90).

Geertz's definition does not need further explanation at this point; I only would like to reiterate that he sees religion as the central symbolic system of a culture. It is worthwhile to focus on the religious system of a culture. What is, in actuality, specific to religion and how does the religious system relate to the other symbolic structures of a given culture? These questions are most relevant in this particular area of research.

Religion as Communication

The anthropologist, Jan van Baal, emphasized the aspect of communication in religious systems. Religion is a system of symbols for communication (van Baal 1981). Religion is in fact communication, as the Latin word

21

religere already indicates since the verb *religere* means to connect, to bind together. It is through religious systems that human beings communicate with the world around them. They feel both a part of the cosmos and alienated from it. As a subject, man experiences a distance between the cosmos and himself and he constantly seeks integration in the whole. He is therefore religious by his very nature.

Humans are both conscious and social beings. As conscious beings, they are aware of themselves. This awareness opens up the possibility of expressing what is felt and thought. Their social nature drives them to express thoughts and feelings. Human beings experience a strong urge to habitually communicate their state of mind to others. For the very purpose of communication, symbolic forms are needed as vehicles to carry messages.

The human being shares his social nature with other mammals. He has a strong drive to live in close contact with other members of his species in family groups as well as in wider social units. Individuals feel an urge to share their experience of life with others and create a common symbolic world where they feel united with one another. Expression and communication are therefore basic human conditions.

Religion and the Search for Identity

Religious systems are used to confirm and reinforce the identity of people. The human being is in search of meaning. He needs to create a symbolic world in which he and the group he belongs to find a home. All communities create narratives about the origins of the group and about the distant past when the ancestors invented and created the basic institutions of the group. People live in a proverbial narrative world. This implies that they tend to create narratives about themselves that provide both spiritual roots and identity. In ancient times a person was part of his kinship group. His individuality was not developed and the group he belonged to by and large determined his identity. Comparatively, people in modern societies have a much higher degree of individuality and privacy. The group determines the identity of a modern person considerably less.

Oral traditions have been instrumental in building up the identity of the ethnic groups of the Ancient Near East. This was also the case with the tribes of Israel. The Biblical texts stem from very ancient oral traditions that served to reinforce the identity of the ancient Israelites.

The Centrality of the Religious System

The religious system is the central part of the symbolic world. It functions as the backbone of the overall world-view of the community and it offers a basic and fundamental orientation towards reality as perceived by a given community. By referring to the centrality of the religious system, I have already indicated what is specific to religion. In addition, I would like to point out yet another element, namely the aspect of transcendence. The

22

religious system entails symbolic forms that refer to a world beyond the empirical world. This is the world of gods, powers, and spirits. Religion can be viewed as a set of beliefs concerned with what lies beyond the empirical world.

The overall world-view that a community holds is composed of a more or less coherent set of representations and beliefs. These representations and beliefs are embodiments of what the community holds as basic truths concerning the world. I have mentioned both representation and belief as elements of a religious system. In order to indicate more precisely what I mean by these two terms, I need to make matters more concrete. I will do this by referring to specific representations and beliefs from the Ancient Near East.

Ancient Near Eastern Cosmology

The cosmology of the Ancient Near East can serve well as a paradigm for a specific set of representations and beliefs. The representation of the world as a three-storied house was widely held in the Ancient Near East. The core metaphor of a house is interconnected with a variety of associated representations and beliefs. For instance, there was the representation of the sun as a personified power responsible for upholding the world. The perception of sunset in the west and sunrise in the east led to the belief that the sun sojourned through the lower story of the building during nighttime and started its day journey through the upper story in the morning. Aside from this, the sun was believed to be the ultimate judge of all people. In the Ancient Near East, the sun was associated with the concept of justice. The lower story, the netherworld, was believed to be the abode of the dead. It was further believed that the deceased ancestors were in contact with the sun in the netherworld. This was a crucial thought. People thought that the ancestors sat together with the sun in a council to judge the lives of the living. Thus the deceased were thought to be in a position where they could influence the lives of their living relatives. It is therefore quite obvious that the cult of the ancestors was linked with basic cosmological concepts.

It was also widely believed in the ancient world that the inspection of the internal organs of a sheep could reveal the hidden causes of misfortune. When animals were sacrificed, the priests or other specialists were reading the signs in the intestines and liver of the sacrificial animal. This practice went back to the universal belief that the sun god used the internal organs of sheep as a writing table. So common ritual and magical practices in the inspection of the internal organs of animals were interconnected with beliefs.

All over the Ancient Near East, people respected their ancestors and honored them with sacrifices. The cult of the ancestors was the heart of family religion. This was also the case in ancient Israel. The sun was not only associated with justice, but also with fertility. Ancestor worship and fertility cults were interconnected in the Ancient Near East. It was also believed that when the moon disappeared each month for three days, it

23

stayed in the netherworld during its absence. The appearance of the new moon was a special moment; the feast of the new moon was associated with particular rites and beliefs related to ancestor worship.

I have made use of two terms thus far, namely, representation and belief. I should like to add that I do not make a clear-cut distinction between the two. It is, however, helpful to use these two terms for different aspects of religious systems. I use the term, representation, to refer to the images people make of the world around them, so it is closely associated with perception. I use the term, belief, to refer to the mental constructs people make about a reality beyond the empirical and, thus it is linked with cognition.

We have seen that Ancient Near Eastern cosmology is made up of interrelated sets of representations and beliefs. This means that the cosmology is the product of creative perception and cognition. The representations and beliefs of a given community are expressed and communicated through symbolic structures.

Religious Texts of the Ancient Near East

When we find ourselves studying an ancient text from the Bible we look at a specific symbolic structure, which is part of much larger symbolic structures. A particular Biblical text refers to representations and beliefs of the ancient people of Israel.

The Biblical authors used "thick" description, local concepts, narrative forms, poetic structures, and metaphors to confirm, to extend, and to modify the representations and beliefs of their time. A modern reader often has great difficulty in finding out what the text is all about, and what the author was attempting to communicate. The reader may not even find enough clues at some places to be able to situate the text within its context.

Characteristics of Ancient Texts

During the last hundred years, archaeologists have discovered thousands and thousands of clay tablets containing a variety of texts written in cuneiform script. These texts were written at the centers of civilization, in Mesopotamia, roughly between 2500 and 1000 B.C. The Sumerians, who created the first city-states in Southern Mesopotamia in the second half of the fourth millennium B.C., invented the cuneiform writing system sometime during the third millennium. Their legacy to humanity contains much more. The invaluable inventions of the wheel, the wagon, the boat, the plough, and pottery can also be accredited to them.

The Sumerians created a very rich and interesting literature. They developed religious structures that have influenced the cultural evolution in the Near East to a large extent. The cosmology of the Ancient Near East is largely the product of Sumerian thought. Scholars are still working on the translation and interpretation of these ancient texts. This is a very

24

complicated and time-consuming task. The ancient texts of the clay tablets are part of a world that is largely unknown to the people of our time. It is, therefore, difficult to interpret this type of text contextually. Ancient texts are often incomplete. The work of the scholar can be compared to a person trying to reconstruct a whole mosaic with access to only a limited number of pieces. These ancient texts provide us with broken off lines both literally and figuratively, incomplete information, and, above all, with many allusions to beliefs and representations we have little knowledge of. The large amount of allusion and the apparent lack of precision are both characteristics of these ancient writings.

Ancient Conventions of Writing

We need to be aware of the ancient conventions of writing texts. When writing systems were first developed, writing was used for recording information rather than for communication purposes. In the temples and palaces of the Sumerian cities, writing was used for the preparation of lists of goods. It can then be said that the list was the first literary genre, in a manner of speaking. Ancient writings often retain and are influenced by the style of a record or list. This is also the case with the Bible. The description of the beautiful temple King Solomon built, which we find in the Biblical book of 1 Kings, do not communicate feelings and emotions to us as modern readers, but rather have the appearance of lists of objects and their dimensions. It is, however, obvious that the author intended to communicate feelings and emotions.

In the ancient world, texts were also recorded for magical purposes. Curses and spells reduced to writing were believed to have more or less automatically an effect even if other human beings did not read them. The prayers and curses written on foundation stones of temples, palaces, and city walls served a magical purpose. They were not meant to be read by people since they were hidden in the earth; they served as magical tools.

Writing for communication developed gradually in the Ancient Near East. The communication of messages became very important when contacts and trade between the cities of Mesopotamia, Syria, and Anatolia developed. The discoveries of the archives of the cities of Mari, Ebla, and Ugarit in recent years have given us many examples of ancient writing for communication. We now have a wide variety of genres at our disposal: treaties, contracts, letters, praise songs, chronicles, epic literature, myths, and legends. However, there are still many clay tablets that have not been deciphered and translated. As far as larger literary works are concerned, we have to turn to the Bible where we find the oldest composite works. The books of the Bible however are ancient books; they differ in many aspects from modern books. Translators and publishers of the Bible need to be aware of the differences between ancient and modern books and should anticipate the problems modern readers have with ancient writings.

25

Ancient Books

Many Biblical books contain typical elements of oral literature due to the fact that these texts pre-existed in oral form and were incorporated in written texts. Folktales, myths, legends, proverbs, folksayings, oracles, formulas of oaths and blessings, prayers, and other forms of verbal ritual appear as oral strata in the written texts. These oral texts have a specific form and structure, and the Biblical authors and editors reproduced these forms literally in their texts. This gives a special flavor to the ancient texts.

It is important to realize that the ancient legends that were at one point incorporated in a larger literary work had a particular status and authority in the community that had created it. People believed that legends revealed important information about the past. An ancient legend often was reshaped by an editor and became part of a larger composition of recounted legends. It retained however a great deal of its original meaning. Many Biblical books are stratified and this complicates the interpretation of the text to a high degree.

Biblical books differ from modern books in many aspects, one of these aspects being structure. Most books in the Hebrew Bible are both compilations and compositions of texts. The book of Genesis is a composition of narratives and many prophetic books are compositions of oracles. A modern reader of a book expects a chronological order and a more or less coherent discourse. Yet most Biblical books lack these features.

Biblical texts feature tremendous amounts of redundancy and repetition. The authors make heavy use of epithets when referring to persons and gods and employ highly formulaic expressions and other types of standard phrases. Redundancy and repetition often have pragmatic and semantic implications, and modern readers who are not used to this specific use of language often misread the text or miss the point the author is making.

Ancient texts reflect modes of thought that are different from the current thought patterns of modern societies. The logical, discursive mode of thought, which is extensively used in modern societies, is not at all dominant in ancient texts. Ancient texts often mirror analogy and association. For example, in the legal texts of the book of Leviticus we find that stains and swellings on human skin and stains on clothes and walls of houses are all referred to as leprosy. Obviously, there is no logical and biological connection between the skin disease and the problems with walls and clothes the text refers to. Hence we are dealing with an analogy. Furthermore, according to ancient thought, swellings and stains were associated with growth and fertility. Fertility is cultic sensitive, so the treatment of stains and swellings on walls, clothes, and human beings called for a similar approach in the ancient culture of Israel (see Douglas 1999:182-185). Translators of ancient texts must be aware that they are dealing with culturally different texts and help their readers to accommodate to unusual and unexpected thought patterns.

Biblical books are not just the fruits of thought of an individual, particular author; they are the fruits of tradition. They thus reflect beliefs and representations of communities. The text of a Biblical book is much less

the individual property of a particular author than is the case in a modern literary work.

Each Biblical book conveys a particular message. A reader must grasp the essence of the message, otherwise he misses the purpose of the book. Biblical scholars often disagree on the main message of the book. Obviously, there is quite a bit of room for speculation. The author of the book is often unknown; this means that the community he belonged to cannot be traced. A further complication lies in the composite nature of the text. The text contains strata from different periods of time. Even more complicated is the significance of the date of publication. When was the book published, what was the role of the editor, and what was the publication strategy behind the actual publishing event? All these questions need an answer in order to obtain clarity about the overall message of the book. When we ask the question when the book of Genesis was published and what the publication strategy was behind the publication, we hear different answers. Mark G. Brett (2000) argues that the publication strategy must be seen in the context of the politics in the Persian Empire. The editors and publishers wanted to counteract the policy of keeping the Jewish race pure from other ethnic groups. The narratives of Dinah, Tamar and Joseph served as a tool for legitimizing the incorporation of foreign ethnic groups into the nation of Israel. I have argued that the core of Genesis was composed, edited and published during the Davidic-Solomonic period and that the book served as a political charter for the United Kingdom in which many different ethnic groups were integrated (van der Jagt 1994). It may well be possible that both points of view can be successfully defended. It may be plausible that an early version of Genesis was published during the Davidic-Solomonic period and a later one during the Persian period, when the entire Pentateuch was published.

High Context and Low Context Societies

The sociologist, Edward T. Hall, distinguishes between high context societies and low context societies. He places the Ancient Near Eastern societies among the high context societies (1976:106-111). Writings produced in high context societies have no clear demarcation between the text and the extralinguistic world of the general culture. Communication to a wide audience is not in focus. Texts are produced for cultural insiders only. These texts contain a great amount of implicit information, missing links, and allusion. Modern western societies are low context societies. Texts written in low context societies must be precise and communicate without ambiguity.

The Hebrew Bible is an example of a high context document. It contains documents that were written in accordance with writing conventions of high context societies. The translator intending to prepare a meaningful translation of the Bible for readers in a modern, low context society is forced to render a considerable amount of implicit information explicit in his translation.

An anthropological approach to the Biblical texts takes the wider context of the ancient text fully into account. This means that the interpretation of the text must be related to the overall culture of the Ancient Near East in general, and to ancient Israelite culture in particular. Since Biblical texts are mostly religious, we must be able to situate these texts in the context of Ancient Near Eastern religions. This implies that we should present a brief sketch of Ancient Near Eastern religions at this point. This is not an easy task, considering that the data of these ancient religions are incomplete and our understanding of the phenomena limited.

The Evolution of Religious Systems in the Ancient Near East

Some historical background

Anthropologists now largely agree that Homo sapiens originated from the African continent. Our early ancestors migrated from East Africa and spread from there all over the world. We can say that the cradle of Homo sapiens stood in Africa. We can also extend this metaphor by claiming that their nursery was situated in the Ancient Near East. There people developed writing systems and religious systems that became instrumental in the further evolution of the human mind.

We have little factual knowledge about the long history of human evolution. We do not know exactly how the growth of consciousness took place, in what phases the evolution proceeded, and what triggered what in the process. The development of language must have played a decisive role. It is through language that the human being can effectively create a symbolic world. The development of a full-fledged language and the discovery of writing down language in a later stage must have been prerequisite for the evolution of religious systems.

The ancestors of the peoples who formed the Ancient Near Eastern societies came from Africa around 80,000 B.C. Sometime around 10,000 B.C., they began to domesticate plants and animals; this is what is commonly referred to as the agricultural revolution. Around 5000 B.C., people started to build walls around their expanding settlements. This development can be seen as the first stage of the urban revolution. Both the agricultural revolution and the urban revolution shaped merging religious systems in the Ancient Near East. Again we must add that we do not have any consistent record of the religious developments and thus cannot resort to more than mere educated guessing.

Between 3000 B.C. and 500 B.C., a rapid cultural evolution took place in various locations in the Ancient Near East: Egypt, Mesopotamia, Anatolia, and the Levant. This cultural evolution gave birth to sophisticated religious systems. The symbolic structures of these systems became instrumental in a further development of human thought.

Early Sources of Ancient Near Eastern Religion

Our sources of the early forms of religion in the Ancient Near East do not provide us with a coherent and complete account. This means we have to reconstruct the religions from incomplete pictures. The literature created by the Sumerians provides us with useful information about the early forms of religious thought. The most relevant texts for research of ancient Mesopotamian religions are the hymns, the epic poems, and the myths. It is enlightening and illustrative to look at one of the very early written sources of the Ancient Near East, the Sumerian epic poems of the hero Gilgamesh.

The Gilgamesh Epic

The Gilgamesh Epic is one of the oldest larger documents of mankind. Most parts of this epic were already written in the first centuries of the second millennium B.C. Gilgamesh, the protagonist of the epic, was the king of Uruk, one of the Sumerian cities. The most complete and probably the latest recension of the epic was found in the famous library of King Assurbanipal of Assyria, who lived in the seventh century B.C. This king collected a vast amount of documents from different epochs in his library in Nineveh, the capital of the Assyrian Empire. The Gilgamesh Epic must have been known in centers of civilization all over the Ancient Near East during the last two millennia B.C., as archaeological findings suggest.

Gilgamesh's search for immortality

The story of Gilgamesh is the story of a tragic hero. Gilgamesh was the legendary founder and king of the walled city of Uruk, situated in southern Mesopotamia. He was two-thirds god and one-third human. His beauty and strength were unequaled in the world. Everything he undertook succeeded. He killed monsters, challenged goddesses, and proved to be on top of all things.

One of the poems tells us that one day Gilgamesh met his equal in strength and beauty in the person of the wild man Enkidu, who lived with wild animals far from the centers of civilization. This Enkidu was brought to Uruk and the two became friends. The story tells us that among other things the two friends killed the monster Hubumba. However, the gods turned against the two friends after Gilgamesh had rejected the goddess Ianna as his bride. They even killed the bull of heaven sent by the offended Ianna to destroy the city of Uruk. It was then decided by the gods that Enkidu, the friend of Gilgamesh, had to die. Enkidu became ill and died. The death of Enkidu caused a crisis in the life of Gilgamesh, as he could not accept death as the final destiny for his friend. He set out on a journey to find the secret of life, the antidote against death. In short, the Gilgamesh Epic harbors all the features of a quest, where the hero of the story embarks on a long and difficult journey in search of something of great value: the plant of life.

Gilgamesh goes as far as the place where the sun sets; he travels through the netherworld up to the fields of gold near the gate where the sun leaves the netherworld in the morning. There he finds Ushnapistim, his ancestor,

the only survivor of the great flood, who has received the gift of immortality from the gods. It is this old man who shows Gilgamesh the plant of life, the plant that gives immortality. After receiving the plant of life, he decides to return home with it. On the way back to Uruk, Gilgamesh unfortunately loses the plant of life. A snake eats it. This tragic loss brings about a fundamental change in the mind of Gilgamesh. He accepts death as his own fate and as the fate of his friend Enkidu. When he returns to Uruk, he has become an altered being; he has changed into a human being conscious of his limitations and reconciled with the fate of death.

The Gilgamesh Epic presents us with glimpses of ancient Mesopotamian religion. The narrative world of the epic is the scene of heroes, ancestors, gods, goddesses, and monsters. Ordinary people do not play a role; they simply serve as background material. Furthermore, it may strike the reader that values are of no particular importance. The world of the narrative is a typically amoral world; neither gods nor heroes are bound to the established moral values of human beings.

The Gilgamesh Epic points out three areas of religious representation: polytheism, the ancestor cult, and the magical world of the monsters. Representations and beliefs in those areas largely dominated the world-view of the Ancient Near East. People lived in a polytheistic, ancestral and magical world. In the Biblical story of the Garden of Eden, we find similar themes and motifs. In Chapter 10 I compare the two stories carefully, as both accounts stem from the same cultural setting and reflect similar thought patterns.

The Sumerian concept and representations of creation

The Sumerian creation theology influenced the thought patterns of the entire Ancient Near East. They invented and developed the concept of a primordial ocean, which existed prior to the creation of heaven and earth. It was the air god Enlil who separated heaven and earth and thus created the world humans live in. The parallel with the first two verses of the book of Genesis is striking (Kramer 1963:1971). In the Sumerian creation poems, creation is thus presented as an act of separation. In some instances it is represented as creation by the word, by divine command, so this too is a concept of Sumerian origin. Also, the more anthropomorphic idea of molding is found in ancient Sumerian creation poems. Man was fashioned of clay and given divine breath by the creator god.

According to Sumerian mythology, the gods decided to create humans in order to be relieved from the hard work they had to perform in order to sustain themselves. The gods retreated at one point from the world and began to live together on the mountain of the gods. This complex of ideas underlies the main representation of the world of the gods. This representation dominated ancient theology and its traces are also found in the Bible. The thought that each god had a special interest in and authority over a particular territory goes back to the time that particular god actually resided in that area.

In the Biblical creation narratives there are significant differences; God created Adam as the one who had to preserve the Garden of Eden, the

garden where the LORD himself walked around in the coolness of the evening. He was not assigned the hard work of feeding the gods, but became a partner of the LORD. Adam represented the God of heaven and earth, not a local god.

The Sumerians developed concepts, representations and beliefs that influenced the religious systems all over the Ancient Near East. The ancient Israelites, who wrote their literature much later than the Sumerians wrote theirs, undoubtedly used Sumerian concepts and ideas in their writings as is evident from the Biblical literature. They resorted to the frameworks of the Sumerians, but also innovated new concepts, enlarged and modified the Sumerian representations, and built a unique theology of creation that we can find in the Bible.

The Polytheistic World-View

In his stimulating book on the history of Mesopotamian religions, *The Treasures of Darkness*, Thorkild Jacobsen sketches the development of polytheistic systems prevalent in the land between the Euphrates River and the Tigris River, roughly between 3000 B.C. and 500 B.C. His work highlights important developments in the growth of human consciousness and is not just a textbook on religion, but also a documentation of the cultural evolution of the human being. Jacobson sees an evolution in the religions in Mesopotamia in particular, and in the Ancient Near East in general. Three main phases can be distinguished. Each phase produced a certain type of gods. These include nature gods, city gods or warrior gods, and personal gods.

Nature gods

Jacobsen relates the earliest forms of religion in Mesopotamia to the growing awareness of human weakness. People experienced an apparent lack of life force and became conscious of their incapacity to rejuvenate themselves. They also became aware of the powerful forces in nature giving birth to all sorts of life. Water and earth, for instance, were able to produce life in great abundance. In the time of spring, new life emanated from these sources and this miracle astonished people from the olden days and filled them with awe. The earth, the sweet waters of the rivers, and the warm rain bringing wind, plants, trees, foods and liquids, such as grain and wine, appeared to be sources of the life force. At a certain point, people began to personify these natural elements and consequently symbolized these in language. As people felt dependent on these personified forces, they began to relate to them in their various forms of worship. Hence the personified natural phenomena became gods. These gods were seen as diffuse and immanent, and generally did not have anthropomorphic features. The representations people made of them were more of a monstrous, anomalistic and bizarre nature, thus lacking the familiar traits of the human being.

It is quite plausible that the invention of gods stems from the personification of natural phenomena, as Jacobsen suggests. Considering the fact that

nature harbors a great variety of forms, it is quite understandable that many different gods came into being. In addition, cultural innovations were interpreted theistically. Each cultural instrument had its specific god who invented it and was responsible for its proper working. For instance, according to Sumerian tradition, it was the god Dagan who invented the plough and oversaw its proper use.

In the Old Babylonian Empire (2004-1595 B.C.), over 2000 gods could be counted. The world of the Ancient Near Eastern people was indeed dominated by hundreds of gods. These gods were not equal. Clearly the god who governed the sun was much more powerful than the one governing the pruning hook. The gods were not operating in the interest of preserving peace and harmony among themselves and among human beings on earth. The ancient mythology reveals a constant struggle for position and power among the gods and quite often the fights between gods led to human suffering. Ancient man lived in a symbolic world in which life was presented as uncertain and fragile. The gods were highly unreliable, moody, and morally unstable. The human being was rendered powerless, at times a toy of the gods and at times a victim of these powers. Thus he was never quite on top of things and in control of his own well-being.

The mother goddess

There is ample archaeological evidence supporting the idea that dating back as far as the Neolithic period, people worshiped mother goddesses. People have attributed supernatural force to the procreative capacity of the woman since the distant past. This force has been personified into representations of mother goddesses. Womanhood and motherhood became metaphors for the forces of life and were associated with fertility, love, sexuality, and the struggle for life itself. Ianna, the Sumerian goddess of love and war, is the oldest example of a mother goddess known from written sources. Her Akkadian name, Ishtar, is attested from later versions in the Akkadian language of the Gilgamesh Epic. Ishtar fell in love with Gilgamesh and caused him lots of troubles in the aftermath of their affair.

We find forms of this type of goddess worship under different names but with similar functions and relationships all over the Ancient Near East. Astarthe, Anat and Asherah are well-known goddesses featured in West Semitic sources. Quite often these goddesses appear as the spouses of the head of the pantheon, although they also function as goddesses in their own right. In many contexts the great goddess is associated with the evening and morning star, Venus. It follows that the title, Queen of Heaven, was often in use to refer to this type of goddess. The cult of the mother goddess was a widespread and popular cult in the Ancient Near East, and it functioned in different forms in a great variety of religious systems and social settings, from Neolithic times to the Roman period. Similarly, in ancient Israel the Queen of Heaven was worshiped. In the book of the prophet Jeremiah the cult of the Queen of Heaven is described as a common practice:

> Do you not see what they are doing in the towns of Judah and in the streets of Jerusalem? The children gather wood, the fathers

kindle fire, and the women knead dough, to make cakes for the queen of heaven; and they pour out drink offerings to other gods, to provoke me to anger (Jer 7.17-18).

City gods

During the third millennium B.C., many more city-states were founded in Mesopotamia. The economic surplus, a result of the successful agricultural revolution, needed to be piled up and securely stored. Walled cities became fortified storage areas, where people also were safe from the attacks of invaders. The third millennium B.C. was not yet the time for the creation of great empires. There were not yet times of peace in large areas for sustained periods as in later epochs. The epoch was one of turmoil and upheaval, particularly because of the frequency of sudden attacks on cities by tribes from the plains and mountains.

This general air of insecurity caused feelings of vulnerability and life was perceived as being precarious. It was held under constant threat, not because of the unreliability of the forces of nature, but because of other people's greed. People living in cities needed additional types of gods and powers, ones who could protect the cities and their inhabitants.

We see that during the course of the third millennium new types of gods emerged. These new gods were portrayed as mighty warriors, protectors of the cities. They possessed particular human traits. They were not human in the sense that they were compassionate and truly concerned with human beings. A city god was a majestic and despotic ruler who owned the city and resided in a magnificent house in the middle of it. He was, in actuality, the god of the city's king before the people. The king was the representative of the city god and his most important assignment was to honor and feed him.

The kings of the ancient Mesopotamian cities were not perceived as normal human beings either. It was believed that they possessed extraordinary powers. Consider, for instance, that Gilgamesh, the king of Uruk, was said to be two-thirds divine and one-third human. We know from the ancient literature that the kings were called sons of gods and appointed as rulers of particular cities by the counsel of the gods.

The worship of the city god was not a popular religion. It was a state affair and the king was the officiator. He could delegate his duties to a group of priests, but he remained personally responsible for the cult of the god. Ordinary people were not allowed to enter the temple, the house of the city god; only the king and the priests could have contact with the protector god of the city.

Personal gods

In the second millennium B.C., a new type of god emerged. Jacobson calls them personal gods. As human consciousness continued to grow, people became more and more aware of their own personality. They began to see their lives as a narrative, as a unique history with its ups and downs, with its luck and misfortune. People discovered their "self" as something vulnerable and fragile. Individuals began to look for patron gods, powers who could protect and bring them luck. Prosperity was generally attributed

33

to the divine. Luck personified as a divine being in the ancient world. In the course of the second millennium B.C., a new type of divine being, the personal god and goddess, emerged.

In religious texts of the second millennium, we notice that the possessive pronoun is widely connected with the divine. Ordinary people speak in letters and prayers of "my god" and "my goddess." Common people refer to gods and goddesses as those who help and support. They are the ones who bring luck. The people of that time could choose their god out of a large group of gods and goddesses. It was often a matter of trial and error. If a particular god or goddess had proven to answer a particular need, an individual could decide to choose that divinity as his or her god. Ancient people attributed their luck or misfortune to their personal deity.

The personal gods were not immanent natural forces, nor despotic divine warriors and rulers, but beings who were concerned with the well-being of individuals. These new gods were concerned with values such as justice and honesty; they felt pity with the suffering of people. They were helpers and saviors of their devotees and truly became gods of justice and mercy, who listened to the prayers of the oppressed and the afflicted. The personal gods became gods of values and people.

The personal gods were very much treated as if they were human parents. The metaphors father and mother for gods occur frequently in the written sources of this period, and this terminology indicates the development of an element of intimacy with the supernatural in the religious thought of that period.

In the second millennium B.C., personal gods became the focus of worship all over the Near East. Written sources from Egypt, Mesopotamia, Syria and the Levant bear witness of this new development.

The Ancestor Cult

Ancestor worship is a universal feature in religions. In many cultures people believe that after death a person undergoes a process of divination. This was also the belief in the Ancient Near East. Ancestor worship in the Ancient Near East was common and interconnected with the worship of gods. The dead were believed to reside in the netherworld, where they were in contact with both the gods of the netherworld and the sun and moon gods, who both sojourned through the netherworld.

The ancestor cult was the core of family religion. By introducing the term family religion, I am turning to a sociological category. At this point I cannot present a full picture of the sociological perspective, but I will deal with this in some detail in Chapter 5. In this chapter I will just underline the importance of the ancestor cult in the Ancient Near Eastern world.

The oldest son of a family, the paterfamilias, was responsible for taking care of the dead. Regular offerings were to be brought to the tombs of the deceased and the names of the dead had to be invoked. In particular, sacrifices to the dead were made during the interlunium, the period between the old and new moon. A sacrificial animal was then killed at the graveside

of the deceased and all the members of the family participated in a sacrificial meal.

The bedroom of the paterfamilias was the principal shrine, where daily rituals were held to keep good relationships with the dead. The dead ancestors were, on the whole, considered to be benevolent towards their offspring, but could, when annoyed, turn into dangerous agents of misfortune.

The Magical World

Magic was a very vital part of Ancient Near Eastern religion. The ancient peoples believed they lived in a world dominated by supernatural powers: divine beings, half divine beings, monsters, spirits, and demons. All these powers formed a constant threat to the good life of the people. The worldview of the peoples of the Ancient Near East can be characterized as magical. In a magical world-view, the world is perceived as a place where there is a constant lack of order and rank. Life is not stable and secure, and anything can happen. People can be transformed into demons, gods can take on animal forms, and so on. Magical potions and fruits can change the destiny of people in an irreversible manner.

In a magical world the causes of fortune and misfortune are difficult to trace as they are hidden beneath the thick veil of ignorance. People in ancient times were simply ignorant of cause and effect patterns in their surroundings. Misfortune, illness, and death perpetually fell upon them, and people continually made attempts to identify the agents of their misfortune. They turned to all kinds of divinatory practices. They also tried to defend themselves at all times by using amulets and other magical means. They attempted to counteract misfortune by engaging in rituals, sacrifices and offerings, and resorted to spells and curses. Diviners, seers, mediums, and magicians held instrumental roles in countering evil, misfortune, and death. Thus they held a considerable amount of power over ancient societies.

The world appeared to be a place of disorder and insecurity caused by a serious lack of structure. Spells and curses seemed to live their own life and were considered irreversible since even the highest powers remained impotent against them. For instance, the highest god could not reverse the curse and blessing of an ancestor lying on his deathbed. The words of a curse or a blessing had magical power that operated independently of other forces and thus could not be controlled by anyone. In the book of Genesis, we read that the blessing of Jacob by his father Isaac was irreversible although he had been mistaken and Esau was the rightful beneficiary of the patriarchal blessing.

Ancient texts often feature magical fruits and potions. In the story of the Garden of Eden, two special trees are introduced, each producing magical fruits. They are the tree of the knowledge of good and evil and the tree of life. Adam and Eve ate from the tree of the knowledge of good and evil and the magic of the fruit transformed them into divine beings (Gen 3.22). The Creator then decided to chase the two away from the tree of life. The

narrator offers the following motivation: if Adam and Eve ate from the tree of life, they would live forever. In other words, the Creator could not have prevented Adam and Eve's immortality if they had eaten from the tree of life. The magical fruit would do its work and even the Creator would be unable to undo the effects of this magic. Magical thought was an important constituent of Ancient Near Eastern religion. Here it is again evident that it is important to distinguish between polytheistic thought and magical thought, although the two thought patterns overlap and complement each other.

The Anthropological Model

In an anthropological approach to the Biblical text, religion is viewed from an anthropological perspective and not from a theological one. It is important to reconstruct what the ancient peoples actually believed, what kind of rituals they used, and what their patterns of thought were.

We need an anthropological model of Ancient Near Eastern religion that can serve as an explanatory model for the interpretation of Biblical texts. Anthropologists see the ancient religion of Israel as part of the culture of the Ancient Near East. We have seen that polytheism, ancestor worship, and magical practices were the main ingredients of Ancient Near Eastern religion. So these elements are the main components of the anthropological model of religion that we apply to the Biblical text.

All religions in the Ancient Near East developed over the centuries and this development can be seen as an evolution. However, this evolution cannot be presented as a unified linear process. Religions are complex; the specific needs of communities and individuals are diverse and produce a diversity of religious phenomena. The evolution of the religion of Israel is a special case within the cultural context of the wider region. The development of a monotheistic type of religion in Israel was a gradual process; it did not eliminate the wide variety of ritual and magical practices at one point in time, although most of these were, in fact, incompatible with pure monotheistic faith. We always need to distinguish between practical and theoretical levels in religions. It is obvious that at a theoretical level, in terms of logic, magic and monotheism are incompatible. In the actual praxis of daily life, emotional needs often have the upper hand on logic and rational thought. As late as the period of the European Middle Ages, magic was still prominent within the context of the monotheistic Christian society although it was theologically incompatible.

36

Chapter 4

The Religion of Ancient Israel

Ancient Israel

A superficial reading of the Biblical books of 1-2 Samuel and 1-2 Kings may create a highly idealized picture of ancient Israelite society. The ideal that is upheld in these books is the dream of a single unified state with a coherent religious system focused on the worship of one God. This picture of a unified state, comprising a number of ethnic groups under one ruler and united in one faith, Yahwism, was, in fact, a far cry from the reality in the pre-monarchic and monarchic periods. A more in-depth reading of the aforementioned books leads precisely to this understanding.

The reality of ancient Israel was a fragmented situation. The different clans and tribes of the Israel had their own religious systems. The religion of the ancient Israelite communities was made up of four complexities: the worship of local gods, the ancestral cult, the cult of the national God, Yahweh, and a wide variety of magical practices. It is safe to say that the unified state and its unified religion emerged as late as the Hasmonean period when Israel was ruled by the high priest (162-163 B.C.).

The authors and redactors of the books of 1-2 Samuel and 1-2 Kings described the history of Israel from a specific point of view. They believed that the history of Israel could be summed up as a progressive corruption. Israel received a unified and pure monotheistic religion in the desert before entering the Promised Land. When they settled in Canaan, they began to mingle with the non-Israelite tribes and their religion became more and more corrupted by elements of the Canaanite religions. This ultimately led to the catastrophe of the fall of Jerusalem and the exile in Babylonia.

The historiographers of the books of 1-2 Kings judge all rulers of Judah according to the Deuteronomistic law. This law prescribed the centralization of the cult of Yahweh. A direct implication of this was the prohibition of sacrificial practices in the sacrificial sites (*bamoth* in Hebrew) in all the villages and towns in the countryside. When a king did not make serious attempts to destroy the *bamoth*, he was regarded as a bad king despite the success he may have had in other areas. The *bamoth* were the centers of both the ancestral cult and the cult of local gods. By focusing on the *bamoth*, the Deuteronomistic author attacked the heart of ancient Israelite religion.

The concept of progressive corruption needs to be modified in light of the historical reality. The long-term development of Israelite religion was not a regression, but rather, an evolution from a polytheistic and ancestral religion towards an exclusive monotheism. This development took place within a period of one thousand years—roughly between 1200 B.C. and 200 B.C. The real breakthrough took place during the exile in Babylonia. It is not possible to give a full sketch of the evolution in this book; we must pay attention however to the basic dynamics of this development.

The Social Settings of Ancient Israelite Religion

Religion functions within a social setting, it serves the basic needs of the members of a given community. We should keep this in mind as we reflect on the religious situation in Israel around 1200 B.C. Israelites then lived in small villages in the central parts of Canaan, scattered over wide areas. There was no central government and no centralized and unified religion. The society they lived in was a small-scale society, centered on the head of the extended family, and the religion they practiced was a family religion. The family religion related to the needs of the extended family. It was centered on the veneration of the ancestors and the worship of the local powers that were held responsible for the fertility and general well-being of the people and domestic animals.

The Cult of the Ancestors

Ancestor worship is a universal element of religion; it is almost as ubiquitous as religion. Also, in the Ancient Near East, it was a common religious feature, and consequently, ancient Israel was not an exception in this respect. In the Hebrew Bible we find almost no trace of the cult of the ancestors. The people who collected, selected and edited the Scriptures of Israel felt embarrassed about the early primitive forms of Israelite religion and cleansed the ancient texts of almost all references to the cult of the dead.

Veneration of the Dead

From the archaeological data available to us, it is obvious that the cult of the dead was a common practice in ancient Israel during the pre-monarchic and monarchic periods. The Biblical texts give clear indications that this cult was part of common religion. Prohibitions to sacrifice to the dead, as found in the book of Leviticus, suggest the existence of the cult. One cannot easily deduce from that type of evidence how common the forbidden practices actually were in post-exilic Israel. The following words of the Deuteronomist reveal that the practice existed in ancient Israel:

I have not offered any of it [the first fruits of my harvest] to the dead (Deut 26.14c).

It is unlikely that some people offered from the first fruits of the harvest to the dead while others did not, bearing in mind that ancient traditional society had a high degree of cultural and religious uniformity. Thus we may conclude that offerings of the first fruits to the dead were a common practice in ancient Israel. It is plausible that the sacrifices to the dead gradually diminished in the post-exilic period as the Torah clearly prohibited the ancestor cult.

Family Religion

It is useful to distinguish between family religion and state religion. The first type of religion consists of rituals that are led by the head of a family and are meant to protect the members of the extended family. The rituals of the second type of religion benefit the institutions of the state, in particular, the royal house, the priestly class, and the royal temple.

In the narratives of the books of 1-2 Samuel, we find clear traces of typical family rituals. In one of the narratives of Saul's anointment as king over Israel, we find traces of rituals belonging to family religion (1 Sam 9–10). The narrator tells us that when Saul was looking for the lost donkeys of his father, he decided to consult the seer Samuel, who lived in the village of Ramah. Saul meets Samuel when the latter is in the middle of a family ritual (1 Sam 9). Samuel is presiding over a sacrificial meal, and in all likelihood he was the eldest living brother of his extended family, rendering him the head of his family. In that capacity he was in charge of the monthly family ritual when the living share a meal with the dead. When Saul appears on the scene, Samuel offers him, contrary to common expectation, the right hind leg of the sacrificial animal. This symbolized that Saul was viewed as being of higher rank than Samuel, as it was the custom that the right hind leg was always given to the head of the family (van der Jagt 1996).

The sacrificial meal in the village of Ramah was held at the local shrine (*bamah* in Hebrew) at the time of the new moon. The appearance of the new moon was a special day for ritual activity. The period of three days between the old moon and the new moon, the interlunium, was a critical time in the perception of the ancient peoples. It was a time of heightened ritual activity (van der Toorn 1996).

As Saul leaves Samuel after being anointed king, he sets out to return to his father's place. On the way home he meets several people on the road who appear to be involved in rituals. He meets two men at the tomb of Rachel. Although the text does not say what the men were doing, we can be sure that their visit was not for tourist purposes. They must have been sacrificing at the tomb of the matriarch. The text further adds without any explanation that the men provide Saul with the information that the lost donkeys have returned to his father's farm. The text does not reveal how

these people had received this piece of information, but one suggestion is obvious. People who went to sacrifice at the tomb of an ancestor often spent the night at the graveside and could receive crucial information from the ancestor in a dream.

Saul continues his journey and meets with three men at the oak of Tabor. These men were on their way to "God at Bethel," as the text states. As Samuel had predicted earlier, these men offered part of their sacrificial gifts to Saul in the form of two loaves of bread. The context suggests that these men were also involved in ritual activity. Karel van der Toorn affirms that special periods such as the interlunium were used for rituals that were related to the family religion. Bethel was undoubtedly a center for a local cult, and the people of the region worshiped the god of Bethel as a local god (van der Toorn 1996:214-217).

The narratives of Samuel give us mere glimpses of the ancient Israelite religion rather than a complete picture. We hear about the sacrificial meals held by the extended family or clan. Also, oracles and divination, cults at local shrines, and other religious features are mentioned in passing. Although we do not find a full description of the actual practices, we get ideas about the religion of the ancient Israelites. As our knowledge is incomplete, we often have to guess about what may have happened. Family religion was focused on the veneration of the ancestors and on the worship of a local god; the latter is often referred to as the *"el* [Hebrew for god] of the fathers." In addition, there were numerous magical rites in use of which we have little knowledge.

Statues of Gods and Ancestors

The Biblical sources are vague about the use of actual cult objects, such as statues of ancestors and gods. In the book of Exodus, we read about the following legal procedures for the incorporation of slaves into the household of an Israelite family:

> But if the slave declares: "I love my master, my wife and my children; I will not go out a free person," then his master shall bring him before God [or, the gods; *ha-'elohim* in Hebrew]. He shall be brought to the door or the doorpost; and his master shall pierce his ear with an awl; and he [the slave] shall serve him [his master] for life (Exo 21.5-6).

This text refers to "the gods" or "God" present at the door of the house. It is most likely that "the door" implies the door of the master's bedroom. The gods were probably statues of gods. The meaning of the Hebrew *ha-'elohim*, however, is somewhat problematic. The word *'elohim* can also refer to the dead (see 1 Sam 28.13, where NRSV has "divine being"). It is plausible that *ha-'elohim* stands for statues of ancestors at the door of the bedroom in this context.

It is also noted that the *teraphim* (NRSV "household gods") mentioned in Gen 31.19-32 are called *'elohim*. Rachel had stolen the gods of her father and was able to hide these in the saddlebag of a camel. We learn that Laban, her father, chased the group of Jacob over a vast distance in order to reclaim his gods. The textual evidence reveals that the objects in question were relatively small but highly valuable. We are, however, in darkness about the precise nature of these statues. Were they household gods, family gods who were believed to protect the family, or were they statues of ancestors? Archaeological findings confirm that small statues, both male and female, were in use in the ancient Israelite houses. We must conclude that statues of gods and ancestors were used in ancient Israelite family religion, but we do not know what role they played in rituals.

Women may have used female figurines in special rites to promote their own fertility. Archaeological findings have provided ample proof that female figurines were present in all Israelites households. These figurines were not just dolls; they may have been images of goddesses or female ancestors (see Mazar 1990:502).

The State Religion of Israel

Family religion functions in the context of family life and family concerns. It reinforces family values and is meant to promote the well-being of the family members. Religious systems are also used to reinforce the political structures of larger groups such as states and empires. These religions are called state religions and the dominant god concept is the one of the national god.

In a state different ethnic groups are integrated under central leadership. The king, belonging to one particular ethnic group, feels a constant need to unify the different groups. He could resort to religious systems in order to foster unity in his kingdom. In ancient Israel Yahweh was worshiped as the God of all Israel and all clans and tribes were called to honor him. Saul and David actively promoted the cult of Yahweh and reduced the cults of local gods and ancestor worship during their reigns. This policy was crucial in the process of nation building. Saul, who was the first king of Israel, promoted Yahwism among the different tribes of Israel with all his might (see van der Toorn 1996:266-286). It may be that originally Yahweh was the family god of Saul's clan and that he was successful in his policy to persuade the other tribes to worship his family god.

The great king Solomon used state religion in the same manner, but he also practiced a different model: state syncretism. This latter model had different objectives, but could be combined with the promotion of a state religion. State syncretism aims at bringing people of different ethnic groups, each with its own culture and religion, into a federal union where the specific religion of each group is respected. It proved to be the right policy for empire building.

The notion that each nation has its own god was universally accepted in the Ancient Near East since the common world-view was polytheistic and

41

ancient Israel proved to be no exception to the rule. The following example from the Hebrew Bible reflects polytheistic thought:

> When the Most High [*'elyon* in Hebrew] apportioned the nations,
>   when he divided humankind,
> he fixed the boundaries of the peoples
>   according to the number of the gods[1];
> the LORD's own portion was his people,
>   Jacob his allotted share (Deut 32.8-9).

This text from the book of Deuteronomy identifies the Most High (*'elyon*) with Yahweh, the LORD. It says that Yahweh had appointed different gods over different peoples. He had chosen himself to be the God of Israel (Jacob). This text reflects the polytheistic world-view of ancient Israel as well as its particular monolatry, which is Yahwism. The Israelites believed that the other gods, the gods of the nations, were lower in rank and less powerful than their own God, Yahweh. However, they did not deny their existence.

Polytheism versus Monotheism

A good number of writings in the Hebrew Bible presuppose a polytheistic world-view. This is remarkable and is quite often neglected as a major constituent of the cultural context of Biblical texts. The Hebrew Bible also expresses an exclusive monotheism. However, an exclusive monotheism is only explicitly formulated in the book of Deutero-Isaiah (Isa 40–55). All earlier writings reflect polytheism as the underlying framework of thought, and later writings assume monotheism, but do not explicitly express it.

An exclusive monotheism denies the existence of other gods. It equally implies a universal concept of God; the only god is the God of all peoples. Israel's monotheism gradually developed through different phases of monolatry. This does not imply that we must think in terms of a unified linear process in time. Some communities may have been forerunners; they may have practiced a monotheistic religion while other groups were still mainly polytheistic in their thought.

Monolatry implies a devotion to one particular god. However, it does not deny the existence of other gods. Monolatry was a practice that was not limited to ancient Israel. The peoples of Moab and Edom also practiced monolatry. It is understandable that the promotion of a state religion often implies a development of monolatry. The Hebrew Bible gives us a full picture of the specific type of monolatry that was part and parcel of the culture of Israel.

The Hebrew Bible reflects the Israelite belief in the supremacy of Yahweh. This supremacy has several aspects that must be considered at this point. First, there is the physical and power-related aspect. Yahweh's might surpasses the strength of all other gods; he is a mighty warrior and none of the other gods can meet his strength. Beyond this more primitive concept lies the aspect of value-related supremacy. Yahweh is a god of

righteousness and justice. He is not like the other gods who have no concern for the weak and the poor in the human realm. He is the defender of the widow and the orphan. In Psa 82 we can find the poetic portrayal of a court case that takes place in heaven. God summons the gods and accuses them of practicing injustice in the lands they are responsible for. The gods are presented as corrupt judges who can no longer be preserved in their function and should be dismissed by the highest Judge. The verdict is quite severe in Psa 82.6-7:

> I say, "You are gods,
> children of the Most High, all of you;
> nevertheless, you shall die as mortals,
> and fall like any prince."

The immortal gods are condemned to death as a consequence of their failure to uphold justice. In the final verse of Psa 82, the psalmist urges the Most High to take over from the gods of the nations and assume the rule over the whole earth:

> Rise up, O God, judge the earth;
> for all the nations belong to you!

The Hebrew Bible gives us the picture of a God who transcends all the powers of nature and the power of the gods. The Most High first appoints gods over the different peoples of the earth and after a time he takes over from them since they fail to execute his plan of salvation for the whole earth. This thought is crucial for the understanding of the overall message of the Hebrew Bible and the New Testament. However, this message only becomes fully transparent in the cultural context of Ancient Near Eastern polytheism.

The Magical World

The ancient Israelites were not modern, secularized people. They lived in a magical world, a world full of demons and hidden powers. It was widely believed that certain people possessed special power and knowledge which ordinary people did not. Power was also believed to be present in particular objects, such as statues of gods, goddesses and ancestors, and in plants and trees. The people of ancient Israel ascribed magical powers to the king as we can conclude from the following text:

> Then David's men swore to him, "You shall not go out with us to battle any longer, so that you do not quench the lamp of Israel" (2 Sam 21.17b).

43

The king by means of his magical powers sustained life in Israel. His death implied more than the loss of a human being; he was considered to be the life-giving light of Israel. The death of a king was seen as a crisis in the Ancient Near East. Life stopped, and nothing would grow until a new king was installed.

The Covenant Box

Another source of magical power in ancient Israel was the covenant box. It functioned as a magical object that could bring disaster to a whole city, as the narrative of the capture of the covenant box by the Philistines reveals (1 Sam 5). In the book of 2 Samuel, we find another narrative that reflects magical beliefs about the covenant box which are difficult to appreciate for a modern reader. When the covenant box was transported to Jerusalem, a man called Uzzah was killed when he stretched out his hand and touched the box to prevent it from falling from the cart during transport (2 Sam 6). These examples reveal the extent to which magical beliefs dominated thought in ancient Israel. The Biblical authors have a tendency to equate magical power with the power of Yahweh, as in the case of the covenant box; its power to kill was ascribed to Yahweh. This is obviously a monotheistic reinterpretation of an ancient magical belief.

The viewpoint that there was no room for any supernatural power besides Yahweh was an ideal that influenced the later editors of the ancient texts. However, it is obvious, even from the Biblical sources themselves, that the mind of the ancient Israelite was dominated by magical beliefs.

Divination

The people of ancient Israel were always in search of knowledge about power itself. Every time disaster struck, the people felt a need to find its cause. Theirs was a magical world and it was never obvious to them what agent had brought about the disaster. In a polytheistic religion there is always the possibility that one of the many gods had become angry because of being neglected. The anger of the gods and ancestors could be evoked by many things and was not just a consequence of an intentional action. A violation of a sacred rule or taboo, a curse, a state of impurity, the neglect of a sacrificial duty, or simply a whim of the gods could result in misfortune, illness or death. The people also believed that the supernatural powers were communicating to them in a mysterious language. They observed nature carefully in order to read the signs. Reading signs, interpreting omens, and consulting oracles were the order of the day, a necessary part of life.

The anger of the gods was believed to be the main source of all misfortune. We should therefore understand that the bulk of ritual was motivated by fear concerning the anger of the gods. The basic operating scheme of Ancient Near Eastern religion can be summarized in three key words: disaster, divination, and atonement.

44

In ancient Israel a great variety of divining techniques were used in order to find the causes of misfortune and illness. In the Hebrew Bible we cannot find any detailed descriptions of these techniques. When the Hebrew Bible refers to divination, often evasive language is used. The authors and editors used generic expressions, such as "to consult the LORD," and one is led to believe that the methods used for divination were the ones prescribed by the Mosaic Law. The Biblical sources refer to the use of the Urim and Thummim (Num 27.21; 1 Sam 28.6; Ezra 2.63) as mediums of divination, as well as the ephod (1 Sam 23.9). However, it is not clear how these tools for divination were used.

In actual practice the people of ancient Israel resorted to the common divination practices of the cultures of the Ancient Near East, as the following text suggests:

> My people consult a piece of wood,
>   and their divining rod gives them oracles.
> For a spirit of whoredom has led them astray,
>   and they have played the whore, forsaking their God (Hos 4.12).

In the post-exilic period, the books of the Torah became more and more the main source to know the will of the LORD. Scripture study gradually pre-empted the need for divination practices.

Concluding Remarks

Ancient Israelite religion was a specimen of Ancient Near Eastern religion. The anthropological model of Ancient Near Eastern religion should be applied to reconstruct the basic structures of this particular religion. A polytheistic world-view, a family religion with elements of ancestor worship, cults of local and patron gods, and a wide variety of magical practices formed the religious context of ancient Israel. However, the religion of Israel also had a unique development. Yahweh became both the personal God of all Israelites and the national God of the entire people. The worship of Yahweh gradually became the dominant force in their total world-view. After the period of the exile, Israel's religion developed into an exclusive monotheism.

The Hebrew Bible reflects the evolution of the ancient Israelite religion over the years. The evolutionary development is not represented in the order of the canon of the Hebrew Bible. The reader is able to discover its traces in the specific language of the different writings. We find a wide variety of metaphors for Yahweh which belong to the different phases of the evolution. Yahweh is presented as a tribal warrior god, as a king, as a husband of Israel, as a caring parent of the individual believer, as a judge of the nations, and as creator of the whole world.

In a historical perspective, we are able to see a blending of several elements. The concept of a personal, loving God, concerned with justice, and a national God of Israel and a creator of the universe are blended into the

concept of a unique, universal, loving God. We find this universalistic concept of God explicitly expressed in Deutero-Isaiah (Isa 40–55) for the first time. This concept is the fruit of a lengthy process of steadily growing religious consciousness, which has its roots in the Ancient Near Eastern culture but grew and found its culmination in Israel. The religion of Israel became a progressive force in the cultural evolution of the human race. It became instrumental to further growth in the consciousness of the human being. We can only understand this when we take the evolution of man as the development of the conscious and responsible self into account. The concept of a universal, value-related God has its counterpart in the human self.

The elimination of polytheism, the denial of the supernatural power of the ancestors, and the reduction of magical practices do not only lead to an acknowledgment of one universal God, but also lead to the acceptance of the responsibility of the self. The human being was viewed as a toy for the amoral gods in the polytheistic world of the Ancient Near East. The individual was regarded as a passive object for the hidden powers and a rather defenseless victim of sorcery and witchcraft. The Biblical account presents us with an image of the human self who is both accountable and responsible for his life.

Notes

[1]There is a textual problem with this verse. I follow the Hebrew reading *bene 'elohim* as the oldest one.

Chapter 5

Honor and Shame:
Core Values in Near Eastern Societies

Social Values

In the previous chapters, I have dealt with religion as a major constituent of the cultural context of the Bible. In this chapter I will look at the social system from the perspective of social values. People's behavior is motivated by values. Humans tend to move towards what is rated as a high value by society and tend to avoid all actions that are considered to have low value or negative value.

In each society there is a basic set of values that dominate social life. For the Turkana people of Kenya, as for many other pastoral groups, they hold that cattle take a very high place in the ranking of values. Every action that is instrumental in adding more heads of cattle to their herd is rated positive among the Turkana. Following this value system, the theft of cattle from other tribes is positive. However, stealing from fellow Turkana is regarded as negative. Cattle herding is more than a mere economic activity; it stands for a complex of values (van der Jagt 1989:9-13).

It is not difficult to discover the core value complex of nomadic pastoral tribes. Understanding the core value complex of a given community is key to the interpretation of their culture. It is therefore essential to pay attention to the core value complex of Ancient Near Eastern societies.

Honor and Shame as Core Values in Ancient Near Eastern Societies

In modern societies it is generally not considered bad or negative if a person openly admits error or accepts defeat in a contest. Even people in high positions can show weakness and may admit errors of judgment or defeat without losing face. Moreover, quite often this is positively rewarded and regarded as a sign of modesty and humbleness. This was not the case in Ancient Near Eastern societies, just as it is not in many other societies in past and present times. In contemporary Mediterranean societies, accepting error automatically means losing out on the honor scale. In those societies honor is the core value and motivates the behavior of all people and

in particular those in high places. Modesty is not among the values that rank high, and showing humbleness does not add to ones ranking.

The reader, *Honour and Shame: The Values of Mediterranean Society*, edited by Jean G. Péristiany, has inspired a group of Biblical scholars in recent years to view the Biblical text from the perspective of social values, particularly from the honor-shame value complex (see Matthews, Benjamin and Camp 1996). These scholars have turned to anthropological research that was carried out in contemporary Mediterranean societies. Needless to say, these contemporary societies are more accessible for researchers than the ancient societies of the Near East. The main assumption that a great deal of similarity exists between the contemporary Mediterranean societies and the Ancient Near Eastern societies has been tested by various studies. Biblical scholars have taken models from Mediterranean anthropology and have successfully applied them to the Biblical text.

Honor and shame can be regarded as being fundamental categories in the value systems of many Mediterranean societies just as they were in Ancient Near Eastern societies. However, we must take care not to erase significant cultural differences between modern societies and ancient ones. It should be noted that whatever brings honor to a person or family in contemporary societies may not necessarily have brought honor in ancient societies and vice versa. We will first look briefly at the honor-shame complex in contemporary Mediterranean societies, and then examine the complex in more general terms.

Honor

What is honor? Honor is the value-rating a person carries in his own eyes and in society. Honor relates to a position on a scale and it can also be regarded as a rank. Honor is attached to individuals and groups such as families and various social classes. It can be attributed to someone at birth and it can be acquired in life. There are two ways to acquire honor. The first way is by living according to certain virtues of which the most important are:

courage for men
purity for women
self-control
prudence
honesty
generosity
knowledge

Honor can also be acquired by challenging others successfully and by adequately riposting the challenges of others.

Honor is considered a "limited good." The term "limited good" is an anthropological concept and refers to whatever is regarded by society as a highly valued and scarce commodity. In some societies cattle are considered

a "limited good," in others cowry shells or money. We need to consider the term "limited good" symbolically. Every member of an honor-oriented society is pursuing the "limited good" honor, resulting in a situation where there is a lot of competition and antagonism.

Challenge and Riposte

The process of gaining or losing honor through challenge is not a random one. One person cannot simply challenge another at any given time. Only people who are on an equal social footing are able to challenge one another. For instance, in medieval Mediterranean society, a nobleman could not challenge a peasant; noblemen could only challenge their fellow noblemen. The rich cannot challenge the generosity of the poor, as they are not on an equal footing.

In honor-oriented societies, people are continually testing one another's abilities, qualities, and knowledge. This means that people challenge one another frequently. Challenges are a fundamental part of social life and much more than mere incidents. People continuously challenge the rank of others and try to move up on the social ladder by defeating a fellow person. Qualities such as courage and generosity and claims of special knowledge are frequently challenged. From the Gospels we know that the Pharisees and scribes challenged Jesus on a regular basis. His knowledge and status as a teacher were tested time and again. He was able to riposte adequately, meaning that his honor was consequently increased and the challengers were often forced to leave the scene ashamed.

Shame

Shame is the other side of the coin. We define shame as sensitivity to the opinion of society or as consciousness of the negative opinion society may hold. Shame is brought upon the person who loses a challenge or a riposte event. These types of events take place in public and the outcome always leads to the public's acknowledgment of the winner. Also, the person who refuses to take up a challenge or who fails to riposte loses honor, and thus brings shame upon himself. Similarly, a person who receives a gift from someone and is unable to return a gift of equal value in due course also brings shame upon himself and his family.

On a larger scale, it can be said that whenever people fail to implement their society's basic values, shame is the result. This often leads to rejection, which implies that society will no longer attribute honor to the person. A person who has been ostracized by his family or society is often said to have died symbolically.

Honor and Shame as Social Categories

Certain physical conditions create feelings of honor and shame. Conditions such as wealth, health, and so on are all symbols of honor, while conditions of illness, nakedness and poverty are all symbols of shame. These physical conditions have become symbols for social conditions.

Honor and shame can be considered universal categories. The honor-shame complex is prominently present in most Mediterranean societies and occurs widely across cultures. The fact that the honor-shame complex is quite ubiquitous can be explained by relating these values to Social Structure, a sociological term that will be explained in detail in the next chapter. Honor and shame are instruments for social rewarding and sanctioning. A person who has acquired honor is rewarded by society, just as the person who is put to shame is sanctioned by it.

However, there is more attached to the honor-shame complex than mere social approval and disapproval. The exchange of honor also proves to be an outlet for frustrations caused by the repressive elements of Social Structure. It gives people the possibility to maneuver within the restrictions imposed upon them. It functions as a clearing house for conflicts and acts in a similar way as scapegoating and witchcraft accusations.

The honor exchange is also the ground on which the secular and the sacred meet. It is there where issues emerge as nonnegotiable, as the ultimate value. Thus in the honor exchange, the ultimate values become sacred. A matter of honor can be considered sacred to the extent of even having to give up one's life for it.

The Mediterranean societies are antagonistic; there is a fierce and constant competition among the male members and between families, which colors daily life. Whether the Ancient Near Eastern societies contained a similar degree of antagonism is difficult to establish. It is, however, already clear from a close reading of some books in the Hebrew Bible, like the books of 1-2 Samuel, that the honor-shame complex played a dominant role in society. A good example is the story of David and Nabal (1 Sam 25). David was challenged by Nabal, humiliated in front of his men, and dishonored. The only riposte for David in this case was killing Nabal.

Shame in the Hebrew Bible

The Hebrew verbal root *b-w-sh* occurs 225 times in the Hebrew Bible. It is used 129 times in the Qal form with the meaning "to be ashamed." The root is used 95 times in the Hiphil form with the following meanings: "to put to shame," "to shame," or "to act shamefully." It occurs only once in the Hitpael form, namely in Gen 2.25. This is the well-known text of Adam and Eve, who were naked but not ashamed before each other. Specific interpretations of this text have colored the rendering of the meaning of the verb here and "shame" has been associated with such components as innocence, sexual ignorance, and sexual purity.

50

In general, nakedness brings shame upon people while clothes bring honor, and in ancient times, refined clothes in particular brought honor to the people wearing them. The root *b-w-sh* is most frequently used in Isaiah, Jeremiah, and Psalms.

While reading through the narratives in books like Genesis, Judges and 1-2 Samuel, it becomes very clear that the notions of honor and shame played an important role in ancient Israelite society. It is also evident that there are many parallels between modern Mediterranean societies and ancient Israelite society, as far as the constituents of honor and shame are concerned. The emphasis on sexual purity for women and on courage and generosity for men are both instances of these important parallels.

Shame in the Book of Joel

The translation of the verbal forms of the root *b-w-sh* causes problems in a number of cases. This is particularly true for its occurrences in the book of Joel. Presently, I would like to refer to an article written by Ronald Simkins in *Honor and Shame in the World of the Bible* (Matthews, Benjamin and Camp 1996). Simkins argues that the notion of shame is crucial for the overall interpretation of Joel. I fully agree with Simkins's claim that the word is a key term in the book.

The situation the book of Joel refers to is one of devastation. The land of Judah was devastated by a plague of locusts and a prolonged drought. It is as if the land was stripped naked; the grain and other crops disappeared completely. This physical condition brought shame on the people. The physical assault of the locusts on the land and the consequent loss of wealth resulted in extreme poverty. Poverty always means shame. However, the most important cause of shame is the inability to give. When someone is unable to give what is owed to another, shame always results. The people of Judah were not able to bring offerings of grain and oil, nor were they able to make wine libations. The temple had to be closed and this was the main reason for their state of shame. The people of Judah could no longer bring the appropriate sacrifices and offerings to God in the temple in Jerusalem because of the extreme scarcity of food. This implies that in the religious-cultural perspective of ancient Israel, God was no longer present among his people, so his people were filled with a tremendous amount of shame. When an important guest is present on a certain occasion, he bestows honor on those who receive him. The presence of God among the people of Israel brought honor to them. The text of Joel alludes to this. When God is present, there is joy among the people because they are honored by his presence, but when he leaves, the joy disappears and only shame remains (Joel 1.12).

Honor and shame always function in a public context. Israel was put to shame in the midst of the other nations. The people of Israel, who claimed to have a powerful and gracious God, had been put to shame before all those who held other claims. The honor-shame situation of the book of Joel has to be placed within the context of a polytheistic world-view. The people of

Israel felt ashamed as they experienced lose. While other people were able to feed their gods and receive prosperity in return, they were unable to keep this up.

Simkins argues that the Deuteronomistic scheme of interpretation, namely the sin-punishment-conversion-restoration-salvation sequence cannot be applied to the reading of Joel. I do not agree with him on this point but would rather assert that the Deuteronomistic scheme needs some modification or contextualization in the book of Joel. It is true that the text does not refer to sin. Apostasy and social injustice are not mentioned as the sins that caused the locust plague and drought. So we are left in the dark as far as the first element of the Deuteronomistic scheme is concerned. The Deuteronomistic call for conversion becomes an admonition to mourn in the book of Joel and this fits the notion of shame. Shame, death, and mourning form a complex. These words are associated with one another. The underlying thought of the discourse is that God is no longer present among his people. This means that shame has replaced joy and the only appropriate reaction, then, is to mourn. The prophet announces that God will return and that he will restore the grain, oil and wine offerings by providing his people with these goods. Then joy and honor will in turn replace shame.

From the above it is clear that only when we apply the honor-shame complex to the interpretation of the message of the book of Joel, the text becomes transparent. Social values are indeed key elements to the understanding of the cultural context of Scripture.

Honor in the Bible

There are a number of specific words in the Hebrew Bible and in the New Testament which are used to refer to the honor concept. These are the Hebrew word *kavod* in the Hebrew Bible and the Greek words, *doxa* and *timei*, in the New Testament.

The noun *kavod* occurs 200 times in the Hebrew Bible. It takes the following meanings:

  heaviness
  greatness
  honor, respect
  glory
  richness
  radiance
  beauty
  power

The Greek equivalent of *kavod* in the Septuagint is the Greek word *doxa*. Out of the 200 occurrences of *kavod* in the Hebrew Bible, the word *doxa* is used 180 times as an equivalent in the Septuagint. In the New Testament we find the word *doxa* 154 times. It means "glory," "greatness," "radiance," "honor," "splendor," or "reflection." The Greek word *timei* is used 42 times

in the New Testament. This word means "price," "value," "honor," or "respect."

Kavod in the Book of Isaiah

Kavod features prominently in the book of Isaiah as the following examples demonstrate:

Then the glory [*kavod*] of the LORD shall be revealed,
and all people shall see it together,
for the mouth of the LORD has spoken (Isa 40.5).

I am the LORD, that is my name;
my glory [*kavod*] I give to no other,
nor my praise to idols (Isa 42.8).

In Isaiah the *kavod* of Yahweh is a key expression. It is the main component of the theological message of the book. The central message in the book of Isaiah relates to the experience of the people of Israel between 700 and 500 B.C. In that period the Northern Kingdom of Israel ceased to exist since it was conquered by the Assyrians in the year 722 B.C. Its population was largely deported. The kingdom of Judah became a vassal state and continued its existence until it fell in 587 B.C.. Jerusalem was taken and part of the population was exiled to Babylonia. The Babylonians destroyed the city of Jerusalem as well as the temple devoted to the worship of Yahweh. This experience caused a crisis of faith in Israel. It was generally believed that the destruction of the temple, the house of Yahweh, implied a defeat of Yahweh himself. The gods of the Babylonians had proved to be more powerful than the God of Israel. The obvious conclusion was that Yahweh had lost his *kavod*. The book of Isaiah, however, contains a number of prophecies that announce a forthcoming revelation of the *kavod* of Yahweh. God will reveal his *kavod* among the nations by saving his people Israel in a miraculous way. He will show that his power exceeds the power of all other gods by delivering his people from the hands of the Babylonians. He will make a straight road through the desert and lead his people back to Israel. In this saving act, his *kavod* will be revealed (Isa 40.5). He will make Jerusalem the center of the whole earth. All nations will acknowledge that he is the only God and will stream to Jerusalem where they will worship the God of Israel and accept his universal rule over all the earth (Isa 2).

Kavod is the specific term used in the Hebrew Bible to refer to the honor concept. The term carries a number of different meanings in different contexts. It is not possible to offer a description of the full range of meanings at this point as this would require an in-depth research that is beyond the scope of our discourse. It is, however, clear that the concept of the glory of the LORD is a central one throughout the entire book of Isaiah. *Kavod* is associated with rank and quality. The *kavod* of the God of Israel surpasses

the *kavod* of all powers and this thought is resonant throughout the book of Isaiah.

The New Testament

In the New Testament, we notice that the Greek word *doxa* takes up a very similar range of meanings. It is also an important New Testament key term. The New Testament writers perceived the life, death and resurrection of Jesus as a revelation of the ultimate power of God. This implied that God received the highest honor through his son Jesus.

New Testaments texts often refer to the *doxa* of God, Jesus Christ, the angels, and the believers in Christ. Since the term can be used both in a more generic and in a more specific sense, the translation of this word is often problematic. A good example is Col 1.27:

> To them [Christians] God chose to make known how great among the Gentiles are the riches of the glory [*doxa*] of this mystery, which is Christ in you, the hope of glory [*doxa*].

Concluding Remarks

Honor and shame were basic social values that dominated the ancient society that produced the Biblical texts. The honor-shame complex provides us with a very useful reading scenario for Biblical texts. When focusing on the concept of shame in the book of Joel, the message of the book falls into the right perspective. By applying the honor-shame complex to the book of Isaiah, the Hebrew term for honor, *kavod*, emerges as the major constituent for the theology of the book. Also, in the New Testament, honor is a recurring and crucial term. We can conclude that the concept of honor with all its implications forms one of the most central concepts in the entire Biblical account.

Chapter 6

Religion and Society

The French sociologist Emile Durkheim (1858-1917) regarded religion as a positive force. He strongly believed that religious systems reinforce the social cohesion in society and are for that reason indispensable. In his view religion was the foundation of any moral order. Well-known anthropologists such as Malinowski, Radcliffe-Brown, Gluckman, Lewis, and many others have followed this line of thought. All these anthropologists emphasized the positive function of religion. They are often classified as functionalists.

The relationships between societies and religious systems are complex. Some parts of the system may reinforce the social and political structures of the society while other parts may express the tension between individuals and the overall structural forces of society.

The functionalists have made a sharp distinction between religion and magic. Religion is seen as a positive social category while magic is regarded as individualistic and antisocial. If the division between religion and magic is indeed a rigid one, as the functionalist presentations indicate, then the result of the research is a fragmented world-view. However, this is highly questionable. It is my intention to come closer to the overall world-view of the ancient peoples as this will allow us to open up the ancient texts we are interested in. My approach to religion is more holistic since it focuses on the human subject and his basic needs. A fragmented presentation of religious systems as mere instruments that foster social cohesion is not helpful in this respect.

In this chapter I would like to take a closer look at the complex relationship between religious systems and social structures in general. A model developed by Turner (1969) can serve us as a guideline. Three of Turner's concepts are of particular value given their usefulness for Biblical research: Social Structure, Communitas, and Liminality. I will now examine these in some detail.

Social Structure

Turner gives a very specific meaning to the term Social Structure. According to Turner, Social Structure exists where human beings live together in groups. The Social Structure forms the proverbial straightjacket

that people live in. It consists of the statuses, roles, norms, rules and institutions that are a part of any given society. These are all symbolic forms that are in use to restrict, regulate, and prescribe people's behavior. It is obvious that in any situation where larger groups of people live together and share common resources, then rules and institutions are a necessity.

Social Structure is considered sacred. It is widely believed that the rules and regulations people have to follow have been preordained and initiated by ancestors and gods. Social Structure always implies restriction on freedom. For instance, females living in certain societies receive a distinct role; they are allowed to perform certain tasks and forbidden to carry out tasks strictly confined to males. The authority of tradition and religion impose prescriptions and they determine prohibitions on them and their lives.

In many societies class membership provides restrictions. For example, a certain person may not be assigned a particular job because of his or her social class. Similarly, a person's age also constitutes rights, obligations and restrictions.

Gender, class membership, age, kinship affiliations, and so on determine what an individual can and cannot do within the society. Rules, customs, norms, and institutions largely restrict an individual's freedom. In modern societies these restrictions have become less rigid as compared to traditional societies, yet even open democratic societies impose a great number of restrictions on the individual.

Turner calls the arrangement of all institutional forms that are operative in a society, the Social Structure. I will employ the term Social Structure based on Turner's definition and, consequently, apply this concept to the ancient societies that produced the Biblical text.

The Durkheimian School of Sociology treated religion entirely as an instrument that maintains Social Structure. Viewed in this light, religion would appear to be a part of Social Structure, that is to say, part of the repressive forces of society. However, Turner holds a different point of view. According to Turner, religion is not exclusively an instrument that reinforces Social Structure; it is also a tool that is used to express an anti-force of Social Structure. The symbolic forms of religion express both structure and anti-structure; the former reflects the order of society, the status quo, and the latter expresses the freedom of the individual. This brings us to the second concept, Communitas.

Communitas

Turner has also coined the term, Communitas, in a specific manner. It stands for the voice of the common people, the individual, and is in juxtaposition to the term Social Structure. The latter always provokes feelings of frustration, resistance, and protest. Social Structure suppresses the basic needs and desires of individuals. The voice of protest rises when the degree of rigidity of the restrictions increases. The voice of protest is, in

Turner's vocabulary, the voice of Communitas. I have borrowed the term Communitas with all its basic connotations from Turner, although I will employ the term loosely and add my own interpretations where I deem it necessary.

People all over the world belong to drastically different cultural worlds, yet essentially they all experience life in a similar manner. Human beings are conscious of their inability to free themselves from the repressive nature of Social Structure. People also find that freedom is one of the highest goods. As a result there is a fundamental tension between the urge to be social and the desire to be free. This tension constitutes the conflict between Social Structure and Communitas. Social Structure always seems to evoke feelings of estrangement from the self, from the inner essence of being. Social Structure threatens the experience of life as a fully human one, as it always pulls and pushes people by means of laws and regulations.

The term Communitas stands for the ideal society where people live together in freedom without tension and conflict. In addition, it can also be defined as true fellowship of equal people. Turner uses the term *Mitmenschlichheit*, borrowed from the German philosopher Martin Buber, as a synonym for Communitas. It is the opposite of Social Structure in the sense that Social Structure threatens Communitas and Communitas rebels against Social Structure. All forms of oppression and inequality among people endanger the Communitas and provoke some form of reaction.

Religious systems therefore symbolize both the structural elements that are operative in the society as well as the powers of the Communitas. They express the tension between Social Structure and Communitas. Whenever Social Structure is symbolized, the need to symbolize the voice of Communitas also arises. We can notice that, historically speaking; great religious innovations have always been triggered by increased tensions between Social Structure and Communitas.

The tension between Social Structure and Communitas plays a significant role throughout the Biblical account; it is yet another key for a meaningful interpretation of Biblical texts.

Liminality

Liminality is another concept used by Turner that is useful in an anthropological approach to the Biblical text. As the word already indicates, Liminality refers to a boundary or threshold. The term points at the ground where Social Structure and Communitas meet. This liminal area can be viewed as a type of battlefield. Liminality refers to a borderline experience. People experience Liminality when they feel confronted with Social Structure and Communitas at the same time. We should not forget that Social Structure, Communitas and Liminality are symbolic forms that function as models of reality. People experience Liminality at certain periods in their lives and at certain places. Some people have a deeper experience of it than others; we could call these people liminal people. They are deeply religious and open for the experience of the ultimate.

57

Some places are particularly suitable for liminal experiences. The borders of rivers, mountaintops, and isolated spots deep in the desert are ideal for hearing the voice of Communitas and feeling the pressure of Social Structure simultaneously. This experience often leads to a crisis in which a new person emerges who may become a founder of a new religion or a revolutionary leader who will rise to oppose the oppressive structures of society.

Liminal people exist in many societies. These people express the voice of Communitas in a very unique way. Mahatma Gandhi in colonial India and Francis of Assisi in Medieval Italy were great idealists and good examples of liminal people. They lived a simple life of modesty and poverty and stressed values such as equality and tolerance. They managed to resist the oppressive powers of the political institutions of their time and helped to build Communitas.

In the Bible we come across a large number of liminal people. We may say that the bulk of the Biblical traditions go back to liminal people. Moses, Amos, and Isaiah, to mention a few of the great Biblical figures, were liminal people who expressed concern for the downtrodden and oppressed and who called for justice and equity, speaking against the established political structures of the societies they lived in.

We can also find groups of people that may be considered liminal communities. These are marginal groups, such as the hippie or flower power movement from the 1960s, prophetic movements throughout history, and the vast variety of sects and cults. Sectarians often take up some of the basic values of Communitas that have been neglected in the official religion. Also, the Jesus movement that existed in the first century A.D. has proven to be a powerful expression of the voice of Communitas (Theissen 1977).

Jesus of Nazareth as a Liminal Person

Jesus of Nazareth has been referred to as a marginal Jew, a liminal personality, who protested against the oppressive powers of the political and religious institutions of his time (Meier 1991, 1994). He was opposed to the rigidity of keeping the law promoted by the religious authorities of his time, and he contested the value of rigid standards of ritual purity imposed on the common people by the priestly class. He warned people against the temptation of wealth and lived a simple life of poverty. We should bear in mind that in Jesus' time fifty percent of the land was in the hands of the rich elite, who were Romans, Herodians and Sadducees, and that the majority of the population lived in poverty. Jesus strove to protect the interests of the poor and downtrodden and was thus challenging the rich and powerful. Jesus was truly a man of the crowds, having left the comfort of his own house and the protection of his family to live his life as a detached person. His genuine concern was intended for those who were weary and carrying heavy burdens (Matt 11.28). One can say that Jesus' Sermon on the Mount (Matt 5–7), especially the beatitudes (Matt 5.1-12), express the value of Communitas. The Sermon on the Mount provides a

blueprint for a society in which the poor in spirit and the pure of heart live a blessed life of Communitas.

When we present Jesus as a mere marginal person or just as a social reformer, we do not position him in the religious and cultural context of his time. Jesus of Nazareth stood in the tradition of Israel's prophets. A particular apocalyptic outlook on history shaped his thoughts and expectations. This apocalyptic world-view must be seen as a particular symbolic structure and as such it merits our special attention. It had grown out of the prophetic movement of ancient Israel and it was further influenced by elements of Mesopotamian, Persian and Hellenistic religious representation. Jesus of Nazareth should be considered a Jewish apocalyptic (Ehrman 1999), as well as a Jewish *hasid*, righteous man (Wilson 1992). He was a person who had devoted his life to the observance and teaching of the law and who was simultaneously an apocalyptic prophet announcing the coming fundamental change in the world: the end of the world and the day of judgment.

The apocalyptic literature we find in the Hebrew Bible provided Jewish communities at the time of Jesus building blocks for a set of specific representations and beliefs, which we call the apocalyptic universe. It is important to look more closely at the symbolic structures of the apocalyptic universe, as it is fundamental in meaningful interpretations of the Bible.

The Apocalyptic Universe

Between 250 B.C. and 250 A.D., a special genre of religious literature developed in Jewish and Christian communities. This special genre is known as apocalyptic literature. The book of Daniel (chapters 7–14) is the best known apocalyptic writing from the Hebrew Bible while the book of Revelation can be considered as the best known Christian work of this genre. The anthology of apocalypses collected in the first book of Enoch, the fourth book of Ezra, and the second book of Baruch are apocryphal apocalyptical writings. We also find many passages containing allusions and references to apocalyptic concepts and beliefs in various books of the Hebrew Bible (for example, Isaiah and Zechariah) and in the Gospels and Epistles of the New Testament.

An apocalyptic writing is a revelation of a secret, divine plan about the future of the world. This revelation is entrusted by a supernatural being, often an angel, to a legendary figure of the past; for example, Enoch, Daniel, and Baruch. These writings are therefore characterized as pseudo-epigraphic.

Apocalyptic literature always contains a message of salvation for the oppressed. It predicts the fall of the brutal powers of the day and announces a glorious future for those who suffer from persecution. Phrased in the symbolic language of the book of Revelation, it reveals the coming downfall of the Beast and the victory of the Lamb.

We can point out a number of distinct elements of an apocalypse: the announcement of a day of judgment for all nations, the coming of a

heavenly, human-like creature or savior, and the return or resurrection of holy ancestors. A final battle takes place between the sons of darkness and the sons of light, between armies of angels and demons. It is followed by the glorious victory of the powers of light, the righteous. At the same time, natural disasters and cosmic phenomena such as eclipses and the ascension of comets occur. All these lead to the final judgment and mark the beginning of a period of bliss.

The role of a messiah or savior is not always a prominent element and is even absent in some apocalypses. The essential components of the apocalyptic world-view are an imminent end of the present world and the coming of a new epoch of abundance and peace.

These beliefs motivated the behavior of members of communities, such as the group of John the Baptist, the disciples of Jesus of Nazareth, and the Qumran sect. The disciples of both John the Baptists and Jesus, as well as the members of the Qumran sect, all formed apocalyptic communities. The followers left their families, jobs and houses and formed religious communities. They believed that they should purify themselves and others for the coming of the end, the day of judgment, and the arrival of the kingdom of God. Both Jesus and John the Baptist preached a baptism of repentance. People were urged to change their lives in order to be prepared for the great day that was near.

The apocalyptic world-view is key to a meaningful interpretation of the New Testament. All the authors of New Testament writings wrote from the perspective of an imminent end of the world. We do not know how widely the apocalyptic world-view had spread among the common people. It is however very plausible that it had permeated the Jewish society at the time of Jesus, and that it was not just the ideology of isolated communities. The hopes and expectations of a new world must have attracted large groups of people.

The Social Context of the Apocalyptic Universe

What leads people to believe that the world they live in will come to a dramatic end and that a new world will appear in its place? What can trigger normal people to leave their families and daily life routine to prepare for a completely different life? The only response to these questions is the consideration of the population's utter dissatisfaction with their present life. The apocalyptic universe was built up over the years with elements from religious representations of ancient Israelite prophets and from Persian and Hellenistic religions, yet it essentially stems from psychologically rooted feelings of frustration and alienation.

From anthropological research we can learn that specific developments in a great number of preliterate, small-scale societies in the South Pacific during the first half of the twentieth century have led to beliefs and concepts that are very similar to the apocalyptic universe of Jesus' time. These societies in New Guinea and from the Melanesian islands were subjected to heavy cultural pressure by the arrival of Christian missionaries

and colonial administrators from the West. Primitive tribes, living in the Stone Age, lost their political freedom and were forced to change their way of life drastically. This meant a serious loss of culture and identity.

After some time the populations in this region began to react in a very strange manner. They began to prepare for the arrival of a new epoch, a time of abundance and bliss. A prophet, who was a charismatic leader, announced the coming of a divine being and the return of the ancestors. Many ordeals and disasters were predicted to occur. People were told to prepare stores and wharves to be able to receive the goods that would be brought by the ancestors. They were instructed to leave their gardens, kill their livestock, destroy their money, and be prepared for the great day. It was believed that all the goods of the whites would be distributed among the people and a time of abundance would begin. The white rulers would be defeated and the old way of life would be restored in a new society of abundance (Worsley 1968).

There are many parallels between the rise of apocalyptic communities in Israel between 250 B.C. and 250 A.D. and the cult movements in Melanesia in the twentieth century. A large part of these common elements can be explained by the existence of a similar social context. Jewish society at the time of Jesus was threatened by a superior power, which colonized the Jewish people and exercised minimal respect for the Jewish identity. The people had lost their freedom as the ruling class promoted Hellenistic culture at the expense of their traditional way of life. The Jewish people experienced a severe loss of identity. This psychological and cultural context fed the people's grand expectations. They anticipated a drastic and dramatic change of the world order and the arrival of a new epoch without oppression and poverty—a time of peace and harmony in a world in which the Jewish people could live undisturbed in the way of their ancestors. It must not be forgotten that the development of the monotheistic faith had formed the culture of the Jewish people in a special way. Apart from the nationalistic component, the monotheistic faith had created a specific identity in Jewish society. The Jewish people felt different from the surrounding cultural environment on the basis of their deviating system of values. The political and cultural oppression by the Seleucids and the Romans inflicted deep psychological wounds. The apocalyptical movements must therefore be seen as outlets for the traumatic experiences the Jewish people underwent in history.

The Apocalyptic Universe as a Key to the Interpretation of the New Testament

All the authors of the New Testament writings wrote their texts from the perspective of the apocalyptic universe. A modern reader who works with a clearly different concept of time and history is in constant danger of misinterpreting the message of the New Testament texts. New Testament authors, such as Paul, were strong believers in the idea that in their lifetime the new world would appear with the Parousia of Jesus Christ. Jesus of

Nazareth, who had risen from the dead, was to Paul the heavenly, human-like savior who would bring about the great apocalyptic change. This deep-rooted belief has shaped all his writing. An example of his apocalyptic mind-set can be found in the first letter he wrote to the Christian community in Thessalonica:

> For the Lord himself, with a cry of command, with the archangel's call and with the sound of God's trumpet, will descend from heaven, and the dead in Christ will rise first. Then we who are alive, who are left, will be caught up in the clouds together with them to meet the Lord in the air; and so we will be with the Lord forever (1 Thes 4.16-17).

Paul believed that he would see the great day of the coming of Christ. He believed that the dead would be resurrected and that he and all Christians would be literally lifted from the earth into the sky to meet the heavenly Christ.

Christian communities in later times had to adjust their belief about the imminent Parousia as time went by and the great day did not arrive. We should keep in mind, however, that the first Christians lived in an apocalyptic universe.

Chapter 7

Ancient Near Eastern Societies

In order to gain an understanding of Ancient Near Eastern societies we can make use of models that have been developed in sociology and anthropology. These models are limited and cannot be considered entirely adequate for our description of the realities of the ancient societies. I am aware that the use of these models may lead to oversimplification. However, they form solid bases for interpretation purposes and, realistically speaking, we have no other alternatives. First, I would like to make use of the models of tribal society and peasant society.

Tribal Society

The model of tribal society can be applied to a vast number of ancient societies in the Near East. The tribal societies of the Ancient Near East were egalitarian in nature. All the members of this type of society shared the same ancestors, were under the same customary laws, and were ruled by a council of elders. In a tribal society, there is hardly any division of labor. For instance, all the members of a given tribal society may be either shepherds or farmers. Thus, there are no distinct social classes and all people are socially equal.

In the Ancient Near Eastern tribal society family, allegiance was of high importance. Ancestor worship and small-scale communal ritual related to the worship of local gods were the basic religious forms. Each village had its local shrine where people brought sacrifices to the local patron god of the village and to the ancestors. The people lived on the land in small settlements or villages and blood ties related all the individuals within the village or settlement to one another. People of one extended family lived together in a village. Members of one particular subtribal unit occupied a larger geographical area.

Israel as a nation did not exist until the time of King David. In the pre-monarchic period, there were a number of tribal societies; for example, the tribal society of Benjamin and the tribal society of Judah. The kings of Israel and Judah developed monarchies in which different tribal societies were integrated. The imposition of new political institutions by the kings often caused tension with the traditional political structures, such as the

council of elders. I will deal with this problem in greater detail later in this chapter.

However, we cannot describe Ancient Near Eastern societies by relying solely upon the egalitarian tribal society model. In addition, we also need to examine a different type of society, namely, the peasant society.

Peasant Society

The peasant society model can be applied to a number of societies in the Ancient Near East. With the urban revolution, a new type of society emerged in the Ancient Near East. The foundation of city-states in Southern Mesopotamia in the second half of the fourth millennium B.C. created a new type of society. This new society was non-egalitarian in nature and was formed by peasants and city people. The peasants lived on the land and survived off its produce. The city people and the peasants were often of a different ethnic group. Family allegiance was not the cement of the peasant society as opposed to tribal society. The city dwellers and the peasants were bound together by their social contract. A peasant could not be considered an entirely free person. He was obliged to sell or donate his crop surplus to the city dwellers.

The peasant society was a class society; the peasants formed the lowest class and the city dwellers were of a higher class. Also, in the city there were different classes. Division of labor stratified the peasant society of the Ancient Near East. In the city one could find merchants, craftsmen, soldiers, priests, scribes, and officials and each group formed a social unit. These units were not based on kinship but were based on economic interest and the possession of privileges and skills. The members of the highest class of the city dwellers had power over the peasants. In general, the peasants in this type of society were dependent on goods and services provided by the city people.

The religious systems of peasant societies were symbolic expressions of the power structure. This was true for the Ancient Near East where peasants were forced to worship the powers of the city; thus their religion reflected dual allegiance. Their prime allegiance was to the powers that protected the family, the clan and the tribe at large; the second allegiance was to the gods and kings of the city.

In the Ancient Near East, all cities were temple cities since the temple was the central social and economic institution. The social and political life was attached to the temple of the god of the city, who was, first and foremost, the god of the ruler. The palace-temple complex served as a system for the redistribution of wealth. The temple and the king received the products from the land and, consequently, redistributed services and special commodities, as well as titles of honor, privileges, and last, but not least, protection against foreign powers.

The relationship between the peasants and the people living in the cities was unequal. The city dwellers, the king, the priests, and the members of the elite considered the peasants of lower status. Despite this inequality,

there was a bond between the unequal partners. This bond is termed a patron-client relationship in sociology. A patron-client relationship is a personal bond between two socially unequal partners.

In the city-states in the Ancient Near East, the palace, the temple, and the elite of the city owned the land. The peasants did not own land and the members of the elite or the lords maintained a personal relationship with the individual peasants who lived on their land. The peasants had to donate a certain percentage of their crops to their lord in the city and the latter protected their interests in return. Their relationship was a personal bond based on loyalty and reciprocity.

Lord-Vassal Relationships

The patron-client relationship existed in various forms and at different levels in the Ancient Near Eastern societies. Also, the lord-vassal relationship between rulers of different cities was similar in character. A vassal had to pay tribute to his overlord and received protection in return. The institute of patronage was very important in the socio-political life of the Ancient Near East.

In the Hebrew Bible, we find a very specific vocabulary that reflects the basic structure of this patron-client relationship. Hebrew words like *chesed*, meaning loyalty, faithfulness or love, and *tsedek*, meaning correct behavior or generosity, refer to qualities of relationships between people who are not biologically related and socially unequal. Also, the vocabulary of the covenant theology in the Hebrew Bible mirrors the patron-client relationship, being a bond between two unequal partners based on loyalty and reciprocity.

Household and Market

The models of tribal society and peasant society cannot cover all aspects of the ancient societies. An additional model is needed in order to relate to the socio-economic life in ancient times more adequately.

The household–market complex, described by Daniel C. Snell (1997:154-158), proves to be a useful model to refer to the dynamics of the socio-economic forces of the societies of the Ancient Near East. A household is a group of people who regard themselves as members of a production unit. In the Ancient Near East, societies were made up of large households. These units consisted of direct relatives, in-laws, and others such as distant relatives, slaves, and servants. Members of a household did not get paid for the labor they contributed to the household. Instead, they received a variety of material and immaterial benefits in lieu of their services. However, it must be stressed that they never received money. The Abraham narratives in the book of Genesis portray life in a household in ancient times.

To a large extent, households are independent and self-sufficient. A household's degree of autocracy depends on the wider society it is part of.

Households can produce for and profit from markets. A market is a system of pricing goods and labor. This system makes exchange of goods and labor between households possible. Goods can be sold and bought, and people can hire workers and be hired. The Ancient Near Eastern societies developed market economies. Markets are volatile; they can expand and shrink over time as they are subject to a great number of social, political and other factors. The household is a stable unit; its participation in markets can vary from time to time. The household-market model proves to be a useful tool to describe the realities of Ancient Near Eastern societies.

Ancient Israelite Society 1250-586 B.C.

Israelites lived in small villages in the central part of Canaan, beginning around 1250 B.C. The inhabitants of a village form a community of people who live together in one location. A village community is an effective social group. The members have frequent contacts, share resources, and cooperate on a daily basis. They normally maintain good relationships, and when peace is broken, they restore peace through judicial means.

The heads of all households meet together in the village council and decide on all village matters. They also act as judges.

A village community is a territorial group. Membership is not necessarily determined by kinship, but by proximity of location. The families who form the village community have chosen to live together. In ancient Israel blood ties related most inhabitants of a village. The households of a particular village were often from the same extended family (*beth-'av* in Hebrew) or the same clan (*mishpachah* in Hebrew). In the larger villages and towns, the households were from the same clan or at least from the same tribe (*matteh* in Hebrew). Extended families, clans, and tribes are kinship groups. Blood ties determine membership in these groups. Common ancestors are the binding element of these groups. All members of these groups are obliged to support one another. They all share the sacred duty to defend the cause of the kinship group; that is, to protect the lives of all, to ensure resources to sustain the group, and to maintain an acceptable position for the group on the scale of honor. The household and the village were the effective social groups an ordinary Israelite lived in. Daily life was determined to a high extent by social interactions within these groups.

The Israelite kinship groups were patrilineal. Only sons inherited from the father, daughters did not inherit. The eldest son was the main heir. Marriage was patrilocal, girls moved to the households of their respective husbands after the marriage ceremonies were completed.

The household is a social and economic unit. It is a wider group than the kinship group family. The Hebrew term *beth-'av*, literally father's house, is used both to refer to the patrilineal kinship group and the household. The patrilineal group formed the backbone of the household. We should understand that family and household do not totally overlap. In-laws, wives, slaves, and servants could all be members of the household, but they did not all belong to the patrilineal family.

66

A household could consist of the following persons: a head of the household, who is the father, his wives, his younger brothers and sisters, nephews and nieces, slaves, and strangers. When children were born in the household, they had to be adopted by the mother of the household, the first wife of the head of the household, in order to become legal children of the household.

The household was the smallest social unit of the ancient tribal society of Israel. Religion was primarily focused on the needs of the household; for example, the fertility of wives, livestock, and fields. The head of the household was the priest who took care of all the ritual actions that were prescribed by custom. The ancestors needed to be remembered through sacrificial offerings, evil spirits had to be kept away, and the local deity in charge of fertility had to be appeased.

In the early days of Israelite life in Canaan, it seems that households worshiped the god of the father, who was the patron god of the household or the village, under the Hebrew name El or Baal. These gods were mostly local deities. It is highly plausible that Yahweh gradually replaced these local deities as the patron god of households, extended families, clans, and villages.

Tribal Societies, City-States, Monarchies, and Empires

The history of Israel can be characterized as an evolution from a loose federation of small-scale societies to a province of a world empire. When the tribes of Israel settled in the land of Canaan around 1200 B.C., they had conquered territory that belonged to a number of Canaanite city-states. They also settled in areas that were not occupied or sparsely occupied.

The tribes of Israel used to live in small villages and townships. All people who lived in a town belonged to the same tribe and often they were all of the same subtribal unit. Councils of elders governed the tribes of Israel. Each area and each town had a council of elders. These councils were very important institutions, both in political and judicial matters. The elders served as rulers and judges in the society. At a certain point, the tribes of Israel felt the need to integrate the different tribes into a nation under one single ruler, a king, who, as chief of all the tribes, could foster unity among the different groups. They wanted to form a monarchy similar to some of the neighboring nations, such as Moab and Edom. Saul, from the tribe of Benjamin, was the first king, but he was not successful in uniting the tribes and could not face the military strength of the Philistines.

Around the year 1000 B.C., the council of elders of Judah appointed David as king and the councils of the other tribes did the same some seven years later. David was able to integrate the tribes of Israel and other ethnic groups into a monarchy. The tribes had never had tribal chiefs before, so the appointment of a king over all the tribes was actually a novelty.

King David imposed forced labor and taxation on the tribes of Israel. He faced strong opposition from the councils of elders, as they felt more and more marginalized. The councils of elders were an institution that was

deeply rooted in the traditions of the tribes. David had to realize that he could not bypass the councils in the process of political decision-making. He was faced with a revolt led by his own son Absalom and was forced to revise his authoritarian approach in governance by involving the councils of elders in his political decision-making and legislation.

King Rehoboam, the son of King Solomon, also ran into problems with the councils of elders when he ignored the advice of the elders to reduce taxation at the beginning of his reign. This move cost him more than half of his kingdom since the northern tribes decided not to confirm him as their king.

The rise of a monarchy in Israel constantly threatened the ideals of the egalitarian tribal society. We should keep in mind that the peasants in Israel were free peasants. Their freedom and independence were however constantly at stake. The kings set up a royal court and created a class of officials and professional soldiers. The city elite proved to be a potential threat for the needy peasant. Although there were no city-states in Israel according to the model of a peasant society as described above, the city of Jerusalem became a royal city with its own interests and political power.

Israel's prophets reminded the people of Israel time and again about the ideals of the egalitarian society. They often warned the rich against the dangers of greed and corruption. When reading the book of Amos, one is left with the idea that the city of Samaria at its height became a city-state according to the model of a peasant society. The rich elite from the city were able to buy up most of the land around the city. The rich, who used false measurements and other dishonest means to enrich themselves at the cost of the poor, robbed the impoverished farmers of their income and crops.

After 700 B.C. the kingdoms of Israel and Judah became increasingly dependent on the world powers of the day. By 722 B.C. the Assyrians put a definite end to the existence of the Northern Kingdom. The kingdom of Judah continued to exist as a vassal state of Assyria and later of the New Babylonian Empire. In 539 B.C. Israel became a province of the Persian Empire and was governed by a Persian appointed governor.

Politics and religion were closely interrelated in the Ancient Near East. When the kingdom of Judah became a vassal state of the Assyrian Empire, it automatically implied that the king of Judah had to submit himself to the divine powers that protected the Assyrian Empire. Submission to a foreign ruler implied a change in religion. New altars were constructed in the main temple in Jerusalem, and statues of foreign gods had to be erected. A rebellion against the overlord, on the other hand, always went together with a kind of cleaning-up operation in the main temple: images and statues of gods then were destroyed and altars torn down. We find many allusions to this type of operation in the books of 1-2 Kings (see 2 Kgs 16, 17, 20).

Religion and Society in Israel

Yahwism gradually became the central religion of the tribes of Israel. It is not easy to describe the historical process behind the adoption of Yahweh as the unique God of Israel. Was the cult of Yahweh primarily part of the

religious system of the monarchy, or did it stem from the traditional tribal backgrounds? Was Yahwism originally a tribal religion of nomadic tribes outside Canaan? Should we interpret Yahwism as the religious system of nomads and peasants and assume that it had its roots in the expression of Communitas, to use Turner's term, or should we regard it as a tool for reinforcing Social Structure?

The experience of the people who were part of the Exodus profoundly influenced the religious thought of Israel. We do not have enough data to describe in detail how this Exodus group influenced all the tribes of Israel. First of all, we are in the dark about the sociological composition of the Exodus group. Was the group a detribalized group of slaves, called Hebrews, who had fled from Egypt and mixed with other groups from Egypt in the Sinai desert? Was Yahweh originally a mountain God from the desert?

The Biblical sources suggest that groups from the Exodus group settled in the Transjordan area and in the central hill country of Canaan. The Levites, who were stern promoters of Yahwism, lived among several groups and may have acted as soldiers of Yahweh. It may be that the groups that originated from the Exodus group influenced other ethnic groups from Israelite descent living in Canaan, and promoted the cult of Yahweh in the midst of local cults. Most questions cannot be answered because we lack the hard data.

Norman Gottwald (1979) interprets Yahwism as a new religious system that acted as a uniting force, unifying several loose marginal groups in the land of Canaan around 1250 B.C., the time of the settlement. He views Yahwism as the ideology of the oppressed and downtrodden. Gottwald describes the formation of Israel as a state in terms of a revolutionary movement of peasant groups. They were originally shepherds and nomads, and were able to liberate themselves from the lords living in the cities in Canaan, around 1200 B.C. At that time the power of the Canaanite city-states declined, creating a vacuum. Thus the rise of Israel as a distinct political and cultural entity was the result of a revolt against the established powers. Yahwism was, in this respect, the common ideology that united the different groups. Gottwald speaks of a retribalization process; he assumes that the peasant societies disintegrated before 1200 B.C. and that a number of tribal groups regained their freedom from the city lords and reorganized their communities according the rules of tribal societies.

Van der Toorn (1996) views the matter differently. He regards Yahwism as the original family religion of the clan of Saul, the first king of Israel. The latter promoted Yahwism as a state religion among the other tribes of the tribal federation. Yahwism was used as a tool that reinforced unity among the tribes. It also served as an instrument to legitimize Saul's supremacy as leader of all Israel.

The pictures Gottwald and van der Toorn present appear contradictory at first glance. However, they can be complementary and equally applicable in different contexts and periods of time. Yahwism as the state religion of Israel was instrumental as a tool to reinforce Social Structure. Yahweh was also the personal God of individuals and groups; he was the one who was concerned with the oppressed and afflicted, thus voicing Communitas.

Role and Function of Yahwism in the Hebrew Bible

When reading the books of the Hebrew Bible, one becomes aware that the Biblical authors often express a tension between the features of Social Structure and Communitas. We are able to detect the voice of Communitas most clearly in prophets such as Amos and Isaiah in their criticisms of the elite in Samaria and Jerusalem.

In the Deuteronomistic works, we find a great deal of reservation with regard to the institutions of the monarchy and the temple cult. There is a strong emphasis on justice and equity, but not on sacrifice and ritual. The ideals of the egalitarian tribal society are constantly upheld. In the books of 1-2 Samuel on the other hand, we find a certain idealization of the royal house of David. There seems to be a contrast between the restrictions the Deuteronomist imposes on the king and what happened in reality. According to Deuteronomy, the king was not allowed to have many horses and wives, but David and Solomon did not follow this part of Deuteronomy. They built armies and organized harems as all Ancient Near Eastern monarchs did, yet the author of the David narrative in the books of 1-2 Samuel almost sanctifies the royal house of David. The Deuteronomistic work on history expresses a certain amount of tension between the Deuteronomistic viewpoint, which is the voice of Communitas, and the forces of Social Structure, which were operative in actual life. The Deuteronomist presented an ideal situation, yet, in reality, things were quite different.

In the Priestly work, we encounter a strong promotion of the priestly ideals of purity and exclusivity. This can be seen as reinforcing Social Structure. So there are different voices in the Biblical account, and the different positions that were taken are all connected with Yahwism. It is difficult to claim that Yahwism is the religion of the peasants, as it is also doubtful to state that it was exclusively a state religion. Yahwism was instrumental in giving voice to Communitas; it also served as a tool for reinforcing Social Structure.

The New Testament

In the New Testament, the most powerful protest against the established forces came from Jesus himself. In his time the peasants living on the land were forced to give half of their crops to the landowners. Peasants were poor and often in need of basic commodities while the landowners, mostly Herodians and Sadducees, lived in excessive luxury. Jesus preached the Good News of the coming Kingdom of God to the poor people of his time. By doing so, he followed ancient traditions of Yahwistic beliefs.

The early Christian communities practiced a form of communal life. The rich sold their belongings and distributed their wealth among the poor people. In this manner the ideal of Communitas was close to realization. The inspiration for this type of life came from the ancient traditions of Israel and from the words and attitude of Jesus.

It is safe to say that early Christian religion functioned as a symbolic system affirming the status quo. At the same time, it was also an instrumental force in liberating people living under oppressive regimes or powers. This means that the same symbolic system was used to express different representations of reality.

Chapter 8

Ritual as a Model of Interpretation

Introductory Remarks

Ritual thinking has left its marks on the Biblical text on many occasions. We can even say that the overall message of the entire Christian Bible can be expressed in ritual terms. This statement certainly calls for clarification and needs to be illustrated with examples from the Scripture. I will do this in the last part of this chapter.

A ritual is a specific tool for communication. It uses acts and gestures, and although oral texts are quite often part of ritual, the main core of the communication structure is not language but instead non-verbal communication. Rituals are often interconnected with myths. In some instances, ritual clearly enacts a particular myth. In a number of cases, one can only discover parallels between the ritual and a particular myth while in other situations, there seems to be no connection to a myth at all. A myth is a sacred traditional story in which deeds of supernatural beings are recounted.

Myths are stories that are set in specific time frames. A number of myths are situated in primordial time. This is the age of beginnings before the normal life of human beings began. These myths are mainly etiological since they explain why things are as they are in the world (see Chapter 10). Rituals that are interconnected with this type of myth are to be repeated time and again, since it is believed that the performance of the rituals sustains the order of the world. Another category of myth is situated on the verge of eschatological time. The eschatological time is the epoch that follows the present time. Rituals linked with this type of myth are believed to advance an ultimate change of reality. A third category of myth is situated in eschatological time itself. Its rituals effectuate an ultimate change in reality.

Ritual as an Instrument for Change

The word "change" is the most generic term that can be used to characterize the message of the Bible. Yahweh, the God of Israel, is a God of change. He changed chaos into order in his work of creation. He will change this

world of suffering back into a paradise in the eschatological time. As an agent of liberation, Yahweh changed the fate of the Israelite slaves who were oppressed in Egypt. The liberation of the tribes of Israel from the oppressive powers of Egypt is described in specific ritual terms in the book of Exodus. The events leading to the Exodus from Egypt are viewed as a transition rite and a sacrificial rite.

Christians have interpreted the death of Jesus as the unique sacrifice that changed the fundamental order of the world. The Gospel writers describe the life and death of Jesus as a ritual. This ritual took place on the verge of the eschatological time. In their perspective it was the prelude to the ultimate change of the world. The early Christians, therefore, were expecting the end of the world within years.

Change and ritual seem to belong to the same domain. Ritual can be seen as a dramatized narration of a change of state and, at the same time, as an instrument of change.

Ritual in the Bible

In this chapter we will apply the reading scenario of ritual to the Biblical text. There are two ritual patterns that stand out in the Biblical text. These are "sacrifice" and "rites of passage." I will deal with sacrifice in connection with myth in the next chapter. In this chapter I will look into the complex of the ritual of passage in some detail, which is not only a universal ritual but also a crucial element in the Biblical account.

The Rite of Passage as a Universal Rite

All over the world across different cultural areas, people perform specific rites that anthropologists call "rites of passage." It was the anthropologist, Arnold van Gennep, who observed that all rites of passage are basically similar in form and structure. In 1909 van Gennep wrote his well-known book, *Les Rites de Passage*, offering a wealth of material on rites of passage across different cultures. Consequently, his book became a classic in the field of anthropology and the term, rites of passage, is widely used by scholars of various disciplines. Also, Biblical scholars have turned their attention to rites of passage. In recent times many studies demonstrate that the Biblical texts have numerous references to rites of passage (see McVann and Malina 1995).

Van Gennep has pointed out that all rites of passage have three phases:

1. the separation from the old status,
2. the liminal or threshold period (the time in between the old situation and the new), and
3. the incorporation into the new status.

The concepts, Social Structure, Communitas and Liminality, will be applied to the rites of passage as these have proved to be appropriate for a description of the specific structures of this particular ritual. First, we will look at some concrete examples of rites of passage.

Initiation of Boys into Adulthood

I am taking the initiation of a boy into adulthood as an example. My short account will refer to the tribal world of Africa. In many tribes all over the African continent, boys undergoing the initiation rite to become full members of their tribal society have to leave their families, and in some cases even the village community, in order to spend a period of time with the other candidates for initiation in seclusion. Often the place of seclusion is "out in the bush." When the boys arrive in their bush camp, they are stripped of all clothing and marks of distinction. They must become physically and socially equal. The boys are often treated harshly during their time of seclusion since this period is a liminal period during which the boys are molded into new beings. During this period they must learn the basic and ultimate values of Communitas. They are often punished, humiliated, severely beaten, threatened with death, and frightened with the awesome powers of the dead ancestors and other supernatural powers. It is the time that the most sacred teachings of the community and the deepest secrets of life are revealed. The sacred voice of Communitas speaks to the young boys, imprinting the sacred values of the community into their lives. In a number of societies, circumcision and subcision of the penis take place during the liminal period. Ritual bathing and confession of sins also belong to the ceremonies and rites of the initiation into adulthood in many cultures.

The third phase, the incorporation into adulthood, takes place within the tribal or village community. The symbolically new-formed persons are given new names and asked to take certain offices. At times they are asked to perform a ritual only adult males are allowed to perform. There are a wide variety of symbolic forms that express the incorporation into the new status.

Initiation of Young Men in Turkana Society

The initiation of young men in Turkana society takes place during a sacrificial meal of the initiated men (van der Jagt 1989:38-41). The Turkana are a pastoral nomadic tribe from northwestern Kenya. They keep cattle, goats, sheep and camels on which they entirely depend for their daily food. On the day of initiation, each candidate has to come to the meeting of the initiated men of the area with a male goat or ox. In front of the initiated men, each young man has to spear the animal he brought as a sacrificial animal, and afterwards he has to share the meat of his animal with all the men in a sacrificial meal. During the meal the following happens:

- Each candidate is smeared with the contents of the intestines of his sacrificial animal. This is a ritual of cleansing.

- The young men are not allowed to speak.

- Each candidate receives three bones from his sacrificial animal and is invited to crush the bones and eat the marrow from them. He pretends not to have enough strength and requests help from his initiation-father.

After the sacrificial meal, each newly initiated man goes to the home of his initiation-father. This man has helped the candidate during the whole initiation ritual. When the two arrive in the home of the initiation-father, the young man is stripped of all his clothing and belongings. His head is shaved and a cap of clay is put on his head. An initiated man can only wear the clay cap. The clay cap symbolizes the supernatural force that is in the earth. This is the force that brings forth, reinforces, and sustains life.

When the young man returns home after staying for some days in the home of his initiation-father, he appears to be a completely ignorant person. He asks the names of all the people and objects in his home, and is given their respective names as if he did not know them.

The Turkana see initiation as a new birth. The actual moment of the birth can be identified. It is during the sacrificial meal with the initiated men. It is symbolized by various elements. The young men are not allowed to speak as newly born babies cannot yet speak. They have to pretend to be without strength as the newly born are weak. When the sacrificial meal is over, they have to pretend that they cannot walk properly and are in need of help. All these elements indicate that the ritual birth took place during the sacrificial meal. The commensality of the sacrificial meal includes the ancestors, who are supernatural in the widest sense of the word. The newly initiated person crosses the boundary between the impotent world of the non-initiated and the potent world of the initiated. A Turkana man is believed to be in touch with the sources of supernatural power from the very moment of his initiation.

The symbolic language of the Turkana initiation ritual shows many parallels with the language of the baptism ritual we find in the New Testament. We will look into this parallelism in more detail later in this chapter.

Initiation of a New Chief in Africa

In some tribal societies in Africa, the rites performed during the inauguration of a new chief are very similar to the initiation rites of the young boys. An interesting case is the inauguration of the chief of the Swazi people (see Kuper 1944). Similar to the initiation of boys, the chief-elect must stay in seclusion for some time. He, too, is subjected to humiliation, beatings, and death threats. It is believed that prior to becoming a ruler, one

must first listen to the voice of Communitas. One cannot be elevated to a high position without being humiliated first. So the chief-elect is made to listen to the voice of the people he is to serve later. The basic values of Communitas, which are also the basic rights of the people, need to be forcefully imprinted into the heart and mind of the ruler-to-be. This is the background to the initiation of new chiefs.

Rites of Passage and the Biblical Text

The symbolic structure of rites of passage is another key to a meaningful interpretation of a Biblical text. This applies to specific Biblical passages and also to the overall Biblical message.

Specific Passages from the Old Testament

I have applied the reading scenario of a rite of passage to the narrative of Job in the second chapter of this book. When applying this scenario to the story of Job, it became possible to understand the major change that took place in Job's life. We saw that the sufferings of Job can be understood as part of a liminal period he passed through. I will now select a second text, this time from the book of Genesis, to demonstrate that a difficult text can become transparent when it is read as a rite of passage.

Genesis 15: The Rite of Cutting in Half and Passing Through

In Gen 15 we find the account of a very special kind of sacrifice Abraham performed when he was "out in the bush." This rite of "cutting in half and passing through" has posed problems for Biblical scholars, and many commentators have had great difficulty in providing a coherent interpretation of this particular ritual. The situation can be described as follows: Abraham kills sacrificial animals and cuts them in half, and with the pieces of the corpses he creates a kind of passage. After a period of waiting, Abraham falls into a deep sleep. Then smoke and fire pass through the passage between the halves. The context indicates that the entire ritual is an answer to a question Abraham poses to God:

> But he said, "O Lord GOD, how am I to know that I shall possess it [the land]?" (Gen 15.8).

The Hebrew word, *y-r-sh*, is translated "possess" in NRSV. It could also mean "inherit" or "conquer." The question that Abraham put forward, namely, how could he know that he would indeed possess the land, is a pertinent one. God told Abraham that he had purposefully brought Abraham to the land of Palestine, and that he would give Abraham many descendants. Furthermore, he would give the entire land to his descendants. The reality

77

then was that the land was in the possession of others, so a transformation of ownership was required. Transformation always calls for ritual in traditional societies where people think ritually. It is unthinkable in the perspective of ancient man that one can just take over someone else's land without performing the appropriate ritual.

In Ancient Near Eastern society, people believed that any time a person crosses a boundary he is obliged to perform a ritual. A boundary is a threshold, and cannot be crossed without some kind of ritual activity. Even the crossing of a river required ritual in ancient days, and people often piled up a heap of stones after crossing a river.

Gen 15 provides us with the rite of passage in which the landless nomad Abraham crosses a boundary and enters a new land ritually, and subsequently becomes a new person. He becomes the legitimate owner of the land. The rite of "cutting in half and passing through" effectuates this entire process of change.

As I previously mentioned, rites of passage always have three phases:

1. the separation from the old situation,
2. the liminal period, and
3. the incorporation into the new situation.

These three phases can be seen in the four acts of Gen 15 as follows:

Act 1: In the initial scene of Gen 15, we find Abraham alone, separated from his family somewhere "in the bush." This context is symbolic for the separation from the old situation. Abraham must take a number of animals: a heifer, a goat, a ram, a turtledove, and a young pigeon. Alone and single-handedly, he kills these animals and cuts them in half. The narrator does not mention the presence of a helper. This is quite significant since the task of killing fairly large animals requires assistance, particularly when the method of killing entails cutting the animals in half.

Act 2: After Abraham finishes cutting the animals in half and laying down the halves to form a passage, he falls into a deep sleep. This was an unusual state of sleep. The text suggests a deep, intense and terrifying darkness descending upon him. The sleep and darkness symbolize the liminal period. During his sleep Abraham encounters God, who speaks to him and reveals important secrets concerning the future. He hears from God that his descendants will be aliens in a foreign country, but that they will return from that country as rich people and will be able to take possession of the land of Canaan. Abraham learns that he will live long and become very old. Thus God delivers a very crucial message during this period of sleep and darkness.

As a result of this rite of passage, Abraham is transformed into a person with knowledge; he changes from a child, ignorant and innocent, into an adult who knows what life and the future entail.

He becomes a prophet, as it were, and all this is expressed in the symbolic language of ritual.

Act 3: Then a new situation emerges: a smoking fire pot and a flaming torch pass through the halves of the dead animals. The smoke and fire are symbols for the divine. God himself passes through the halves and enters, albeit symbolically, the land of Canaan, thus taking the land into possession. The LORD God becomes the owner of the land, which previously belonged to foreign nations. We must keep in mind that in the Ancient Near East, it was believed that gods owned land and that the people living on that land had to feed their gods from it. In Gen 15 the LORD, the God of Abraham, takes possession of the land that belonged to the gods of the Kenites, the Kenizzites and others.

Act 4: As soon as the LORD took possession of the land, he entrusts the land to Abraham. We read:

> On that day the Lord made a covenant with Abraham . . . (Gen 15.18).

The overlord God gives the land to his vassal Abraham, and the two enter into a covenant relationship.

The Symbolic Language of the Rite of Passage

Most commentators interpret the rite of "cutting in half and passing through" as a covenant ratification rite. It is assumed that the rite establishes the relationship between God and Abraham. The fundamental problem that arises is how to interpret the fact that God himself passes through the halves and not Abraham. The one who passes through the halves takes an oath in the usual covenant ratification rite; he expresses in a symbolic way that he too will be cut in half like the animals if he breaches the covenant. It is almost inconceivable that the text expresses this thought. It is as if God takes an oath and says, "The same will be done to me in the event that I do not keep the covenant." The rite of "cutting in half and passing through" is used in the Ancient Near East as a symbolic instrument to establish covenant relationships. However, the same ritual is used in different situations and the symbols are polysemous.

O. Masson describes a Hittite ritual used for the purification of an army (1950). When the Hittite army was defeated, a special ritual had to be performed. A man, a male goat, a young dog, and a young pig were killed and the bodies were cut in half. The whole army had to pass through the passage formed by the halves. They also had to pass through two fires and through a doorway made of wood. After this, they were all sprinkled with water. The Hittite rite is clearly a purification rite.

The Turkana of northern Kenya continue to practice very similar rites to the one described in Gen 15 (van der Jagt 1983:64). Before setting out for a cattle raid in the area of a neighboring tribe, the Turkana men consult a diviner who gives instructions that the men must follow in order to ensure a successful raid. They are often told to kill a human, to cut the corpse in half, and to pass through the pieces with the cattle they capture from their enemies. In this Turkana ritual, purification and transfer of ownership are effectuated by a rite involving "cutting in half and passing through."

In Gen 15 we are presented with the rite of "cutting in half and passing through" in the context of the transfer of land ownership. It is obvious that the rite of "cutting in half and passing through" is part of the symbolic language of the larger structure of a rite of passage. Different contexts create different meanings. However, the main issue is the aspect of change. A child cannot change into an adult unless a ritual is performed. Similarly, a defeated army cannot fight again and be victorious unless the soldiers are transformed from losers into winners. A landless nomad cannot possess the land of foreign people unless the appropriate ritual is performed.

The Life of Jesus as a Rite of Passage

The life of Jesus, partially and as a whole, is described in the Gospels in the symbolic language of rites of passage. In Luke 3–4 we find a description of the transformation of Jesus from a carpenter's son into a prophet. The baptism in the Jordan River, the period of seclusion and temptation in the desert, and the entry into the village of Nazareth, where he reads the Scripture for the first time, are all instances that can be related to the three stages of rites of passage. During Jesus' life we can see another change taking place. Jesus, the prophet, changes into the Servant of the Lord and becomes a liminal person to whom the sacred powers of the divine are revealed in a unique way.

The Gospels reveal that Jesus, in the course of his trials, is separated from society and from all human contact. He is even abandoned by his own disciples and ends up entirely alone, dying on the cross. In the liminal period of suffering and death, however, the ultimate powers of life are bestowed upon him; he becomes the Lord of all.

The Christian Language of the New Testament

In the New Testament, we find a specifically coined language that is used to describe a new reality and a new experience of life. In the Epistles the Greek word for new, *kainos*, is used frequently to refer to the new reality of faith in Christ. In one of the letters of Paul we read:

> So if anyone is in Christ, there is a new [*kainos*] creation: everything old has passed away; see, everything has become new! (2 Cor 5.17).

80

The emerging of a new reality of existence out of the old is a change. People experienced this change in their lives as a true *metanoia* (Greek for "change"). This change caused by faith in Christ has been described with the symbolic language of rites of passage. The Christian language of the New Testament makes heavy use of symbols related to the rite of baptism. The rite of baptism was the initiation rite of the Christian community. The particular symbols of baptism are concerned with the metaphors of death and rebirth. Becoming a Christian was perceived as a process of death and rebirth. Many concrete examples can be quoted of specific Christian language that makes use of metaphors taken from the symbolic patterns of rites of passage. A text from Paul's letter to the Galatians is one example:

> As many of you as were baptized into Christ have clothed yourselves with Christ (Gal 3.27).

This particular text evokes the image of the initiated who are stripped of their clothing in the liminal period and are given new clothes as they enter the new society as newborn people. A modern reader of the New Testament can only understand this type of language when he or she interprets these words in the light of rites of passage.

As I stated before, the meaning of the Greek word *kainos* has specific connotations derived from the language of rites of passage. The early Christians experienced life as a new experience of Communitas. When people became Christians, they felt liberated from the restrictions and limitations of ancient religious laws and from the obligations of ethnic adherence. They felt that they now belonged to a new cosmopolitan society which had not existed in any form before.

Chapter 9

Myth as a Model of Interpretation

We have already examined a number of reading scenarios for Biblical texts in the previous chapters. Finally, we apply the reading scenario of myth. Reading scenarios can often function as explanatory models and this is particularly the case in the scenario of myth. Myth is a powerful tool for communicating meaning. It has been universally used to express the most fundamental elements of a people's world-view. Myth and fundamental truth are intrinsically interconnected. We should recall that a myth is a special narrative in which supernatural beings play a significant role. The model of myth can lead us to the message of the entire Bible, as it sums up the narrative of the experience of human beings with the Creator from the beginning to the end of time.

Girard's Approach to the Bible

The French literary critic and historian, René Girard, has used the myth of the scapegoat as a powerful explanatory model for literature from all over the world. He has also analyzed a number of Biblical texts. He regards the universal myth of the scapegoat as the main explanatory model for the entire Bible. Some of his insights are valuable for our research and helpful for a further exploration of a mythical reading of Biblical texts.

Girard has developed a reading scenario for the Biblical text that has fascinated many people. Numerous symposiums and special issues of scholarly journals have been devoted to Girard's work. Reading Girard is almost as difficult as reading the Bible. Girard has contributed to a wide range of fields, such as psychology, literature, the Bible, the history of religions, ethnology, and so on. Let me present a brief overview of the main thoughts Girard has brought forward.

The Violent Nature of the Human Being

According to Girard, people are essentially violent in nature. It is in the very nature of a human being to desire what another person possesses. Desire is the driving force in humans. Girard points to the fact that desire

is mimetic in the sense that people constantly copy the desire of others. This is true for all humans in both the past and the present, in Girard's perception. Mimetic desire is a basic condition of human beings.

Girard further believes that a particular experience mankind had in primordial times has determined human thought. It is retained in the myths of all peoples and can be found in many great works of literature. This great and tragic experience of the early man is also reflected in the Bible. However, Girard believes that this great traumatic experience and the distortion of human thought that resulted from it have found a solution in the Bible. The Biblical account puts an end to the veneration of violence, which is characteristic for all myths. It describes the end of violence, which entails the end of sacrifice, as it abolishes the universal glorification of sacrifice and opens up a new chapter in the spiritual evolution of man.

Based on his insight that the Bible is unique among all sacred scriptures of the world, Girard became a Christian. It should be noted that he rejects the interpretation of the death of Jesus as being a sacrifice.

Freud and Lévi-Strauss

Girard builds on ideas held by scholars such as Sigmund Freud and Claude Lévi-Strauss. Drawing on Freud's theories, he formed the hypothesis that religion originated from a traumatic experience of early humans in primordial times. In Freud's *Totem und Tabu* (1913), he describes a situation in primordial times in which the father and head of the family held exclusive rights over all the female members of the group. One day the sons revolted and killed the father. This murder caused serious feelings of guilt that still haunt men until the present, according to Freud. The sons started to worship the slain father some time after the murder and institutionalized the incest prohibition and the rule of exogamy. Religion, according to Freud, originated from a traumatic and violent act that was committed in the primordial past, so it has its origin in crime.

Girard took up the Freudian theory on the origin of religion and modified this theory slightly. This brought him to the following scenario: In primordial times, violence threatened the evolution of the human race. Mimetic desire featuring extreme rivalry rendered it impossible for people to live together and cooperate. Once, in primordial times, people selected someone out of their midst and turned against that person. He was selected on the trivial basis of some abnormal physical trait, but was otherwise innocent. People blamed this person for all wrongs and killed him. They turned against him with force, and in doing so they were able to channel their aggression in one particular direction. As soon as the person was killed, the anger and aggression faded away and life could continue. Soon thereafter, people became conscious that the death of the victim had a very positive effect on life since it brought peace. So they projected the positive effect of the killing on the slain victim and began to worship the victim. Consequently, the innocent victim, killed by society, became sacred. Girard

calls the above sequence of acts the mechanism of scapegoating. The victim killed by society was a true scapegoat.

Scapegoating as a ritual entered the human subconscious in primordial time. Human beings found an effective method of channeling aggression and of protecting society. All peoples on earth have developed a myth of the beneficial death of the scapegoat. The myth of the scapegoat has become part of the cultural heritage of the human race. The enacting of the myth in the rite of the scapegoat was instituted as a fundamental ritual. The original murder committed in primordial times became a sacrifice in the ritual interpretation, and sacrifice was universally accepted as the ultimate necessity of life. The rite of the scapegoat became a cultural universal.

The myth of the scapegoat can be found all over the world and in all the great literature. It is important to note that the scapegoat is always a disguised character in mythological narratives; therefore, it is not always easy to identify the scapegoat among the characters of the story. Girard's method for the analysis of myths can be characterized by the attempt to unveil the true identity and intentions of the characters.

The anthropologist Lévi-Strauss argues that all myths can be traced back to a single myth (1958). According to Lévi-Strauss, one can discover the basic pattern of all myths by finding rules of transposition and simplification. This process is often called the reduction of myths. The themes of all myths can be reduced to one if the language of myths is understood. Myths speak a special language and one can only access this language with the aid of a decoding device. For Lévi-Strauss the basic pattern is the opposition of culture and nature. Girard also applies reduction to his interpretation of myths; he sees the scapegoat mechanism as the basic theme of all myths.

Jesus as the Scapegoat

Girard interprets the life of Jesus in terms of the universal myth of the scapegoat. The Gospels reveal that Jesus was a scapegoat who was the innocent victim of the violent crowds. The Gospel narrative makes it very clear that all people turned against him, including his own disciples. However, the Gospels condemn the murder of Jesus, pronouncing it illegal, false, and devoid of reason. They point at man's violent nature and expose the scapegoat mechanism.

Girard is convinced that all myths disguise the truth about the scapegoat, and only the Gospel writers play a new and unique tune. They condemn the violence and inform the reader that the death of Jesus was truly a crime since there was no legal ground to convict Jesus. Other New Testament writers interpret the death of Jesus as a sacrifice, but Girard rejects this interpretation vehemently. He deems it backsliding to the primitive thought of a God who wants to kill innocent victims.

Girard sees scapegoats in all the Biblical stories and discovers the specific language of the universal myth of the scapegoat in every text. I do not follow Girard in this respect. However, I do believe that a mythological reading of a large number of texts helps us to discover specific textual features. The

idea that all Biblical myth can be reduced to a single universal one is a distortion of the rich variety of texts we find in the Bible. We are presented with many instances of typical mythological language in the Bible, where the mythological themes and motifs featured can only be interpreted within the symbolic system of myth. Girard's work can help us identify and interpret significant mythological themes and motifs in Biblical texts.

Girardian Reading of Biblical Texts

Girard identifies a number of structural principles at work in Biblical texts. These principles are like underlying concepts that are part of the deep structure of the text. Three structural principles are prominent in the approach of Girard. These are mimetic desire, sacrificial crisis, and foundational violence. The story of the death of Abel (Gen 4) presents us with a good example of where these three structural principles can be clearly distinguished.

Mimetic Desire and Sacrificial Crisis

In Gen 4 the narrator introduces two brothers who were remarkably different. One is Abel, who was a shepherd, and the other is Cain, who raised crops. Cain was the older of the two. The narrator informs the reader that the LORD was pleased with Abel's offering but not with Cain's. This situation provoked mimetic desire. Cain desired what his brother had obtained and what he had not received, namely, the favor of the LORD. According to Girard, mimetic desire always leads to a crisis situation and this, in Girard's terms, is a sacrificial crisis. Cain killed his brother who was an innocent victim; he sacrificed a scapegoat. In Gen 4.8 we read:

> Cain said to his brother Abel, "Let us go out to the field." And when they were in the field, Cain rose up against his brother Abel, and killed him.

The theme of murdering a brother is a recurrent one in mythology. The narratives in the book of Genesis are not pure myths. The narrator recounts myths, but also adds other elements, such as etiological asides and theological and ethical comments. This is also the case with the Cain and Abel story.

Girard sees the ethical comment as an integral part of the narrative. In fact, he regards it as the major constituent of the intended meaning of the story. The ethical comment in this narrative is expressed in the form of a question. Directly after the murder, God addresses Cain with the question: "Where is your brother Abel?" (Gen 4.9).

The Biblical text of Genesis reproduces mythological themes, but always situates the mythological in an ethical and theological framework. Cain is held responsible for the murder he committed. Abel is a scapegoat, killed as

an innocent victim. The murderer is guilty of a crime and this is explicitly signaled in the text. Here Girard highlights the crucial difference between myth and Biblical recounted myth. The Biblical author breaks with the primitive thought of the scapegoat myth. The language and logic of the myth is interrupted by an ethical comment, which transposes the original myth into a Biblical anti-myth.

Girard compares the story of Cain and Abel to the story of Remus and Romulus in Roman mythology. Romulus killed his brother Remus and the city of Rome was founded on the blood of the brother. Girard notes a significant difference between the two myths. Remus did not respect the limits of Rome; he was a transgressor in the mythological context. Abel, in contrast, was a completely innocent victim.

Foundational Violence

The violence in the story of Cain and Abel is foundational violence in Girard's terms. The crime leads to the birth of the people of Cain and the foundation of the first city. The latter seems to be an important innovation. One could ask the question whether the main title of the myth should not be the foundation of the first city, rather than the murder of Abel. This probably goes too far and only links the foundational violence with a particular cultural innovation. It may be that the report of the foundation of the first city was added as an etiological aside to the story. It is a recurrent motif in myth that violence gives birth to innovation. The narrator of the Genesis stories makes extensive use of this motif, as we will discover later on in this chapter.

A text like the story of Cain and Abel should, in the first instance, be interpreted within the mythological register since it is a story written in mythological language. Girard is fully aware of this and offers an interesting exegesis of the whole story and, in particular, deals with delicate questions, such as the issue of the mark on Cain.

The Mark on Cain

After murdering his brother, Cain receives a mark that distinguishes him from others. This has puzzled many commentators. It is obvious that the mark is a mythological sign. Girard relates the mark to the danger of mimetic desire. The mark clearly indicates that the bearer is different from others and that the distinction is one to be respected. One should not desire whatever it is the bearer of the mark possesses.

The sociological background of the story is the historical hostility between the nomadic herdsmen and the agriculturists who became sedentary and city dwellers in the Ancient Near East. The agricultural revolution and the development of urban culture led to conflict and tension on a large scale. The story of Cain and Abel reflects this tension.

Conflict and Violence in Genesis

The book of Genesis is a book full of violent conflicts. When we look carefully at these conflicts, we can detect a pattern: all conflicts are the result of attempts made to erase fundamental distinctions. The crisis caused by the attempt to erase a fundamental distinction is solved in a violent manner, either by destruction or by expulsion. Adam is expelled from paradise, Cain driven from the fertile land, and Jacob driven out of Canaan. Abel's life is destroyed, the whole earth is flooded, and the cities of Sodom and Gomorrah are set on fire. The violence in Genesis is functional just as it is foundational; destruction and expulsion have to be interpreted as mythological motifs.

The Narrative of the Garden of Eden

In the story of the Garden of Eden (Gen 2.4–3.24), it is the distinction between gods and human beings that is in danger of being erased. When Adam and Eve eat from the forbidden fruit, they become like gods. The distinction between humans and gods becomes obscure and this constitutes a crisis (see Chapter 10 for a more detailed analysis).

This crisis is solved by their violent expulsion from the Garden of Eden. Mythological creatures with deadly weapons are placed at the gate of the garden to bar the road to the tree of life. The paradise story is, in actuality, a violent one. The violent expulsion from the garden is foundational violence and it is highly innovative. The expulsion from the garden is the foundational myth of the human race. Adam becomes a tiller of the soil, which means he is the inventor of the domestication of plants, the first farmer. Eve becomes the mother of all human beings. She is the mythical pioneer of childbearing and childbirth. The first human beings leave paradise and set out on their journey through time.

The Narrative of the Great Flood

The story of the great flood (Gen 6–9) features the same mythological motifs as the story of the Garden of Eden. The sons of God take women from the sons of men as wives. The distinction between gods and humans is erased. The children born out of the marriage between the divine beings and the humans are giants (*nephelim* in Hebrew), who begin to terrorize the earth with violence. A crisis builds up, leading to the divine decision to destroy the whole earth by an enormous flood.

The Narrative of Lot and the Destruction of Sodom and Gomorrah

The episodes of the destruction of Sodom and Gomorrah along with the incest of Lot and his daughters (Gen 19) form one narrative (van der Jagt

1994). The first scene of the narrative is within the city of Sodom. This city is a very strange place since all the men in that city are homosexual. Lot has two daughters, but the text suggests that the men of Sodom are not really interested in women. Although Lot has two sons-in-law, they are not attached to his daughters and they do not play any role in the narrative.

When two male visitors come to Sodom, all the men in the city want to have sexual intercourse with them. The two men had come to Sodom to warn Lot about the coming destruction of the city. God had decided to destroy the city since it was a place of sterility and violence. The two visitors rescue Lot, together with his wife and two daughters. They flee the city that is bound for destruction by fire. The sons-in-law remain in the city.

The second scene of the narrative is the flight from Sodom to Zoar. On the way to safety, Lot's wife disappears. She looks back at the city in flames and becomes a pillar of salt despite the warning issued by the two rescuers. The disappearance of Lot's wife is part of the mythological logic of the narrative. This logic calls for a situation where Lot ends up with his two daughters as the only survivors of a disaster.

The third scene of the narrative is in a cave in a mountainous area. The text suggests a shift in time. Lot and his daughters are now pictured in primordial time. The narrator suggests that they were the only living humans on the surface of the earth. The older daughter turns to the younger one and says:

> Our father is old, and there is not a man on earth to come in to us after the manner of all the world (Gen 19.31).

Lot is pictured as a patriarch without a successor, which is a very familiar theme in the book of Genesis. As in so many instances in the Genesis narratives, the women are the ones who take the initiative to break through an impasse. The daughters trick their father by giving him a lot of wine to drink, and when he has become drunk, they sleep with him. The patriarch is presented as passive without will and resolve. He simply drinks the wine, becomes drunk, and fulfils the role of procreator in an incestuous relationship without knowing it.

The incest motif occurs in myths all over the world. Incest is a type of foundational crime in mythology, which is directly related to creation and innovation. Gods, legendary ancestors, tricksters, and others commit incest and, as a result, things are created. The earth, the sun and the moon come into place, new ethnic groups are founded, new plants discovered, new instruments invented, and institutions innovated.

In some African traditional societies, prospective rulers were obliged to commit an act of incest before they could be installed as king. For instance, this was the case among the Swazi of South Africa (Kuper 1944). The incest act committed in this context is believed to have a special effect on the prospective king, as it removes him ritually from the ranks of the ordinary people and bestows supernatural powers on him. These powers make him fit to rule. However, the crime of incest he committed needs to be dealt with and someone must die in the place of the king.

There is a universal taboo on incest in the world, but in myth incest is a foundational motif.

In the story of Lot, we deal with mythological incest. Both daughters become pregnant and give birth to sons. The oldest daughter calls her son Moab, which sounds like "from my father" in Hebrew, and the younger one calls her son Ben-ammi, which means "son of my relative" in Hebrew. The name-giving openly demonstrates that the sons are the fruit of an incestuous relationship.

The incest of the legendary ancestor Lot leads to the birth of two new ethnic groups: Moab and Ammon. The author of Genesis has treated the incest story in its category as a legend of an ancestor. He abstains from any moral judgement since he understands the mythological meaning and logic of the narrative.

Judah and Tamar

The story of Judah and Tamar (Gen 38) resembles the narrative of Lot in many aspects. The patriarch Judah, as in the case of Lot, is bound to die without a successor. Although he himself had three sons, one son after the other dies under suspicious circumstances without producing an heir. The oldest son, Er, married a Canaanite woman by the name of Tamar; he died unexpectedly, without leaving children behind him. The narrator informs his audience that the LORD killed him because he was a wicked man. The second son, Onan, inherited the wife of his brother, but did not fulfil the duties of a brother; he refused to impregnate his sister-in-law on behalf of his deceased brother. The narrator tells us, "But since Onan knew that the offspring would not be his, he spilled his semen on the ground whenever he went into his brother's wife, so that he would not give offspring to his brother" (Gen 38.9). The LORD also killed Onan since he was unfaithful to the law of Levirate marriage.

Judah had only one young son left and was afraid of the dangerous woman Tamar, the Canaanite witch who had killed two of his sons already. An anthropologist recognizes the situation immediately. If two young men married to the same woman die suddenly, there is only one suspect in the society—it is the woman. She cannot escape being accused of witchcraft in a society where belief in witchcraft is prominent. We should notice that the narrator knows that it was the LORD who killed Er and Onan, but Judah, the main character of the story, did not know this. He suspected Tamar and sent her back to her father to live in his home. He attempts to save his last son by not giving him to Tamar, his widowed daughter-in-law. By doing so he creates an impasse. Tamar is the matriarch and the successor should come from her in the same way that Abraham's successor came from Sarah.

Also, in this story it is the woman who takes the initiative to break the impasse. Tamar tricks Judah by disguising her self as a prostitute, and has sexual intercourse with her father-in-law, so that she has children. In this case it is not the incest taboo that is violated, but the father-in-law taboo is

broken. In many societies all over the world, the father-in-law and mother-in-law taboo regulates social and sexual behavior. Also, the Torah explicitly condemns a sexual relationship between a daughter-in-law and a father-in-law (Lev 18.15).

It is remarkable that the narrator does not make any moral evaluation. Judah praises the deed of his daughter-in-law. He admits that she was more loyal (*tsedek* in Hebrew) than he had been (Gen 38.26).[1]

Tamar is a trickster-like character. The trickster figures in folklore and mythology all over the world. Tricksters can be humans, both male and female, divine beings, or animals. The trickster is a creator of beings and things. He or she transforms, distorts, and inverts reality. The trickster is able to turn tables in difficult situations. The trickster often finds himself or herself against the odds. By using deceit and ruse, by flouting rules, and by other similar actions, a way out is found. Then a new rule is established, a new being or thing created, and life is preserved. Philip Noss (2001) rightly points out there are a good number of trickster-like characters in the Bible (for example, Abraham, Rebecca, Jacob, Job, and Samson), but a full-fledged trickster can not be traced in the Biblical narratives. Tamar has many traits of a trickster character; against all odds she manages to turn tables.

The story of Judah and Tamar goes back to an ancient tribal tradition of the tribe of Judah. Tamar the matriarch is pictured as a heroine who reversed an impossible situation into a life-giving one. The mothers and grandmothers must have told these stories to the children as these types of stories helped the young ones in their search for identity. The author or redactor of the book of Genesis may have included this story in his book for political purposes. It links the tribe of Judah with Canaanite clans in the region of Adullam. It is highly plausible that the core of the book of Genesis was written during the Davidic-Solomonic period. The time of the undivided monarchy was a period of unequaled expansion in the history of Israel. Many neighboring tribes were made vassals and many ethnic communities were incorporated into the reign of David. Ancient people interpreted political configurations in terms of family relations. Abraham was seen as a father of many nations by the author and compiler of the book of Genesis. His book could serve as a political charter that legitimized the political status quo of the Davidic monarchy.

Legend and Myth in Genesis

The Genesis narratives contain a great deal of recounted legend and myth. Legends are stories that take place in distant times when the ancestors founded the groups. All peoples preserve stories about their ancestors. The ancestors are never dull or colorless; they are often heroic and true legends. They did great things, invented all kinds of instruments, and instituted important rules and customs. All this also applies to the patriarchs and matriarchs of ancient Israel. They too were legendary figures that were not bound to the same norms and rules of ordinary people. They

possessed supernatural powers and strength (Gen 20.17-18; 29.10), had incestuous relationships (Gen 20.12), and were extraordinary people in more ways than one.

Myths are stories about primordial times. They may also recount ancestor stories, but these ancestors are more distant than the tribal ones. An anthropological approach to the Genesis narratives interprets the Biblical text as recounted myth and legend. Evidently the mythological themes and motifs have been used to build a wider theological discourse. This is already visible in the Bible itself and is elaborated more in Christian theological traditions. We can only conclude that an anthropological approach is instrumental in discovering the most primitive layers of meaning hidden in the text and it is as an extremely valuable tool in Biblical exegesis. The translator of the Bible must recognize the typical mythological language of specific passages and respect the linguistic register of myth in his translation.

Notes

[1]The translation of the Hebrew word *tsedek* with the English equivalent "righteous" does not convey the notion of loyalty and faithfulness. Tamar, who was a Canaanite was more loyal to the tribe than the patriarch Judah himself.

Chapter 10

An Anthropological Reading
of the Garden of Eden Narrative

An anthropological reading of the narrative of the Garden of Eden distances itself from the Jewish and Christian interpretations that have been developed over the centuries and attempts to go behind these interpretations to divulge earlier layers of meaning in the story.

The narrative of the Garden of Eden is a recounted myth that must have been known in ancient times in various oral forms. The written version we find in the book of Genesis has etiological asides as well as theological comments that were added in later periods.

Themes and Motifs

The main theme of the narrative is a common one in mythology. Many ethnic groups tell the story of how the first people on earth failed to gain immortality. This is essentially the story of how death came into the world. In many myths the story of how the first people lost a golden opportunity to live forever by making some trivial error is told. Also, the role of a trickster is recurrent in these myths. A large variety of these myths feature a snake that is similar to the one in the Garden of Eden. It spoils the human race's chance of ever becoming immortal and joining the gods.

Myths often contain recollections of a very distant past. They reflect basic psychological traits of the human soul. Taking this into account, it is noticeable that many myths contain elements about the fall of mankind. Humans fell from being friends of the creator to alienation and moral decay. This type of myth reveals a fundamental moral weakness in human beings.

The myths of death and life often have a main theme and a number of subthemes and asides. The narrative of the Garden of Eden is not an account of a single myth. Rather, one is able to recognize many subthemes and asides with distinct etiological purposes.

The Scene of the Garden

The first people, Adam and Eve, lived in a garden in the mythological East. The earth outside the garden was uninhabited and barren. Adam and Eve were living like innocent children. They did not wear clothes and they had not yet discovered their nakedness. In the language of the myth, this actually means that they did not have sexual intercourse. Adam and Eve did not cultivate the soil; they enjoyed a life free of burdens and hardships. The two were placed in a garden full of fruit trees and their only duty was to guard the garden. They could freely eat from the trees, and the land they lived in was a place of abundance.

The narrator tells the reader that in the middle of the garden there was a special tree, a magical tree: the tree of life. The fruit of this tree contained the antidote for death. In many myths there is a tree or plant of life which can provide the gift of immortality. We are also told that there was another magical tree near the tree of life; this was the tree of the knowledge of good and evil. This tree produced forbidden fruit, the fruit that caused death. Hence, there were two trees: one giving life and the other causing death.

It is important to realize that the fruit of both the tree of the knowledge of good and evil and the tree of life was perceived as magical fruit in the original mythological context. Ancient people believed that when someone ate magical fruit that person was transformed into a different being. The underlying thought is indeed magical; it was believed that even the Creator could not undo the effects of the magical fruit. When Adam and Eve ate from the fruit of the tree of the knowledge of good and evil, they became gods, as the text indicates (Gen 3.22). The Creator then decided to chase them away from the tree of life for the simple reason that if they had eaten from the fruit of that tree they would have been transformed into immortal beings.

An Ancient Jewish Legend

The narrative of the Garden of Eden does not give any indication of time. Did the two live in the garden for a long time or was it only for a short time? Ancient Jewish legend claims that the two lived in the garden for a long time and that after many years Adam started to show signs of weakness. Eve set out for the middle of the garden to pick fruit from the tree of life since she felt that Adam was in need of the antidote for death. As she tried to reach the tree of life, she had to work her way past the tree of the knowledge of good and evil, which had formed a hedge around the tree of life. So the tree of knowledge was actually barring access to the tree of life.

When Eve was near the tree of life, a serpent approached her and spoke in a human voice: "Why do you not take a fruit from the tree of knowledge, if you eat that fruit you will become like gods (*'elohim*), you will know what they know and have what they have, you will become immortal as they are" (similarly Ginzberg 1992:38-40). The ancient Jewish legend is particularly

helpful for an anthropological reading as it reflects a more original text with less theological interpretation.

Parallel Stories from Africa

There are many parallels between the Biblical narrative of the Garden of Eden and African myths on the origin of life and death. The similarities are striking, as the following examples will demonstrate. These examples are all single myths, although some have an aside.

The Chameleon and the Lizard

The Margi of the Central African Republic tell the following story. When Death first entered the world, men sent the chameleon to find out the cause. God told the chameleon to let men know that if they threw baked porridge over a corpse, it would come back to life. But the chameleon was slow in returning and death was rampant in their midst, so men sent a second messenger, the lizard.

The lizard reached the abode of God soon after the chameleon. God, angered by the coming of a second messenger, told the lizard that men should dig a hole in the ground and bury their dead in it. On the way back the lizard overtook the chameleon and delivered his message first, and when the chameleon arrived, the dead were already buried.

Thus owing to the impatience of man, he cannot be born again after death (Beier1966).

The Chameleon and the Snake

The Vute of Cameroon have a similar story. God sent the chameleon to the people with the message that they would rise to life after death. The chameleon was very slow and wasted a lot of time on his journey from God to the people. The snake had overheard the message God wanted to convey to the people, so he went to the city and pretended to be a messenger of God with the bad news that people would die and not return from death. The people believed the snake. When the chameleon finally arrived, they did not believe the good news he brought.

The Vute use this myth to legitimize their habit of killing snakes immediately when they see them. They say they have the right to kill them instantly since the snake brought death to their ancestors (Sieber 1925).

Many myths harbor some kind of misunderstanding or mix-up that has caused death to be a permanent condition among people. Often, this misunderstanding is related to a trivial error. Sometimes this error can be traced back to impatience, curiosity, or simple greed. The motif of forbidden fruit also occurs in the myths of African people, as seen in the next myth.

The Forbidden Fruit

According to the Efe of Congo, God created the first human being with the help of the moon. He kneaded the body out of clay. He then covered it with skin and finally poured blood into it. He called the first man Baatsi. God whispered into his ear, telling him to beget many children, but he imposed the following rule: from all the trees you may eat, but not from the Tahu tree.

Baatsi had many children and he made them to obey the rule. When he became old, he retired in heaven. His children obeyed the rule and when they grew old, they too retired in heaven.

But one day a pregnant woman was seized with an irresistible desire to eat the fruit of the Tahu tree. She asked her husband to pick some for her, but he refused. When she persisted, her husband agreed. He crept into the forest by night, picked the Tahu fruit, peeled it, and hid the peel in the bush. But the moon saw him and told God what he had seen. God was so angry that he sent death as a punishment on men (Beier 1966:63).

The Gilgamesh Epic

In the Gilgamesh story, the hero finds the plant of life described as "the secret of the gods." The thorny plant grew on the bottom of the sea, and Gilgamesh managed to get it by tying heavy stones to his feet that dragged him down to the deepest part of the sea. When he took the plant in his hands, he cut the stones from his feet and the sea carried him on the shore. Gilgamesh intended to take the plant to the city of Uruk, where he would give it to the old men. But when he took a bath in a well of cool water, a serpent snatched the plant away, so he lost the antidote for death in a moment of carelessness.

Immortality as a Lost Chance

Humans have been obsessed by their condition of mortality since the awakening of consciousness. All myths express in different ways that by some tragic event the first people lost a golden chance either to gain or to keep immortality.

In universal mythology, gods are immortal and men lose this condition as a result of some kind of mistake or misunderstanding. They are tricked by a false messenger, become the victim of a slow one, or are otherwise deceived. Death is never attributed directly to the Creator; he is never depicted as the one who designed this condition of mortality. All myths of this type contain some element of a theodicy.

The story of the Garden of Eden tells us how the ancestors of the human race lost the golden opportunity of gaining immortality. They lived in a garden with the tree of life at hand. They were very near it, but they could

never grasp its fruit. A snake confused them and they reached for the wrong tree.

The Serpent

Anthropologists are usually not too surprised to find a snake in the Garden of Eden. The snake is used as a universal and polyvalent symbol in mythology. It is associated with procreative power, with both destructive and healing power, and with fertility and wisdom. In Mesopotamian religions, the snake is associated with a range of deities and demons. Some gods are depicted as having a lower body in the form of a snake. Also, the Egyptian pharaohs and gods were presented as having venomous snakes as part of their bodies to protect them. The snake appears in the world literature in a variety of roles: as a deadly adversary, as a trickster, as a messenger of the gods, but also as a healer and a protector.

Scholars of ancient Mesopotamian religion are familiar with the image of a winged creature, a demon, which serves as a guard for the tree of life. On reliefs in Assyrian palaces and temples, we find demons next to the tree of life. These demons are often pictured while picking a magical fruit, which is the date fruit in Mesopotamian mythology. The demons are to feed the king with the magical fruit, but they also have to keep intruders and thieves at a distance. Their task is to tend the tree of life and protect it.

The snake next to the tree of life in the story of the Garden of Eden was not a normal snake. It could speak and it had legs. The text of Genesis clearly implies that the snake walked on legs. When it was cursed because of its role in deceiving the woman, it had to crawl on its belly forever as a punishment. So we must conclude that it was originally a demon with snake-like features, protecting the tree of life.

In the story of the Garden of Eden, the snake takes on the form of a trickster and is the personification of confusion. It blurs fundamental distinctions between humans, gods, and animals. The snake speaks the human language, knows the secrets of the gods, and is, as such, the ideal messenger between the Creator and human beings. However, the serpent is not presented as a messenger, and it is never officially introduced in the narrative. It pretends to be a divine messenger that speaks on behalf of the creator God and proves to be false messenger.

You Will Be Like Gods

In Gen 3.4b-5 the trickster snake said to Eve:

> You will not die; for God knows that when you eat of it [the tree of the knowledge of good and evil] your eyes will be opened, and you will be like God [or, gods; *'elohim* in Hebrew].

The Hebrew word *'elohim* is a plural form, which can have both a singular and plural meaning. It can mean God or gods here. The word *'elohim* is used as a personal name for the Creator and as a class name for divine beings in the Hebrew Bible. The narrator of the Garden of Eden story always uses the compound name, Yahweh Elohim (LORD God), for the Creator when he speaks himself. The snake also uses *'elohim* to refer to the Creator. However, in the clause, "you will be like *'elohim*," the term is used in a different sense, namely as a class name for divine beings. In this context it is unlikely that *'elohim* refers to the Creator. The snake does not want to say, "You will be Elohim, the Creator." The Creator is a unique being. The snake predicts that Adam and Eve will become like gods; this means they will share the same characteristics.

Later on in the narrative, Yahweh Elohim says, "See, the man has become like one of us" (Gen 3.22). The narrator confirms that the snake's prediction has indeed come true since Adam and Eve have become like divine beings. How the two have become like gods is a crucial point in the interpretation of the story.

Exegetes of this passage often have been in a bind about what to take literally and what to take metaphorically in the discourse. It is obvious that only when we use the reading scenario of myth, we can make sense of the typical mythological language of the story. We have to respect the register of myth and interpret the mythical motifs within context. This equally applies to the expression, "eating of the fruit." The question that comes to mind is the following: what do eating of the fruit and becoming gods imply? Once again, we should look closely at the text:

> But the serpent said to the woman, "You will not die, for God [*'elohim*] knows when you eat of it your eyes will be opened, and you will be like God [*'elohim*], knowing good and evil." So when the woman saw the tree was good for food, and that it was a delight to the eyes, and that the tree was to be desired to make one wise, she took of its fruit and ate; and she also gave some to her husband, who was with her, and he ate. Then the eyes of both were opened, and they knew that they were naked; and they sewed fig leaves together and made loincloths for themselves (Gen 3.4-7).

In this passage we encounter a number of metaphoric expressions: "eating of the fruit of the tree of the knowledge of good and evil," "opening of the eyes," "becoming wise," and "knowing one's nakedness." All these metaphoric expressions need a contextual interpretation within the register of myth. The discourse is dominated by the verbs "to know" and "to see," and these verbs take up a very specific meaning in the story.

The verb "to know" in Hebrew has a wide range of meanings; for example, it can carry the meaning of sexual intercourse, as it does in Gen 4.1. The suggestion that eating the fruit of the tree of the knowledge of good and evil is a symbolic expression for having sexual intercourse has already been made in patristic literature, so it is not a novelty in the tradition of interpretation. There are a number of clues in the text alluding to the

existence of an associative relationship between the eating the fruit of the tree of the knowledge of good and evil and the act of sexual intercourse.

The narrator tells us that the woman saw that the tree of the knowledge of good and evil was good for the purpose of making someone wise. Wisdom should not be understood as intellectual wisdom in this context since the reference is to practical wisdom. A wise person knows about life. The wise person is the opposite of the inexperienced, innocent person. Adam and Eve were innocent; they lacked the wisdom of life. When they looked at the tree and saw that the fruit of the tree could make them wise, they desired to become wise. Innocent people do not know the ways of procreation; they lack this essential wisdom. The fruit of the tree of the knowledge of good and evil is a symbol for sexual knowledge; it contained the secret of procreation.

The verb "to see" in Hebrew also has a wide range of meanings. It can mean "to recognize," "to understand," "to perceive," and more. The narrator informs the reader that after having eaten the fruit, the eyes of both were opened. In other words they saw and they understood. It is not said explicitly what they understood, but the context strongly suggests that they understood the nature of sexual intercourse. This suggestion is strengthened by the expression, "they knew that they were naked." Eating the fruit brought the immediate awareness of nakedness. The Hebrew expression, "to uncover the nakedness of someone," which occurs frequently in the Hebrew Bible, means to have sexual intercourse with someone. When the narrative speaks about the opening of the eyes and the awareness of nakedness, we have to interpret this metaphorically and relate the meaning to the sexual domain.

Eating the Fruit, Becoming Wise, and Being Like Gods

In Genesis the concepts of eating the fruit and acquiring wisdom are in consequential order. Herbert C. Brichto points out an interesting parallel in the Gilgamesh story, where becoming wise and being like gods is depicted as the result of engaging in sexual intercourse (1998:87).

Enkidu, the great friend of Gilgamesh, used to live with wild animals before he became friends with Gilgamesh. He ate the food of wild animals and was untouched by human culture. He was an innocent wild creature who did not know the ways of sexual intercourse. His life changed when he met a prostitute and engaged in sexual intercourse with her. The sexual intercourse made him a human being; it made him wise. When the change had taken place, the prostitute addressed him with the following words: "Thou art wise, Enkidu, art become like a god" (Pritchard 1969:75). Why did the prostitute call Enkidu "wise" after he had learned the ways of sexual intercourse and why did he consequently become like a god in her eyes? We should understand that ancient people believed that gods were the creators of all forms of life, not humans. Procreation was the prerogative, par excellence, of the gods. This parallel from the Gilgamesh Epic gives further evidence that wisdom and divine qualities were associated with sexual intercourse in the mythology of the Ancient Near East.

Main Theme

The main theme of the Garden of Eden narrative is the loss of immortality and the discovery of procreation. Adam and Eve became wise; they became like gods as they began to create life. Procreation was a quality attributed to gods. It was originally not within the ability of humans, but they learned the ways of the gods by eating the forbidden fruit, which was an act of stealing. Stealing is a recurring motif in many different myths.

Procreation and mortality are mythologically interconnected. When Adam and Eve had eaten from the tree, they became like gods in a specific sense—they learned the ways of procreation. In Gen 3.22-23 we read:

> Then the LORD God said, "See, the man has become like one of us, knowing good and evil; and now, he might reach out his hand and take also from the tree of life, and eat and live forever"—therefore the LORD God sent him forth from the garden of Eden, to till the ground from which he was taken.

Adam and Eve ate from the tree of the knowledge of good and evil. The fruit of this tree gave them the knowledge of good and evil. The expression, "good and evil," should not be taken literally. It is an idiomatic expression that refers to completeness and essence. It allows for the suggestion that nothing is excluded. Thus, these words do not contain moral connotations in this expression. Adam and Eve became like gods, knowing good and evil in the sense that they acquired the knowledge of the essence of life, which is the secret of procreation. They did not acquire the other important divine quality, namely, immortality.

Etiological Asides

In the Biblical narrative of the Garden of Eden, we also have a number of etiological asides. Etiological narratives provide explanation and/or legitimization. These narratives explain why things are as they are and/or why people are authorized to do what they do. One example of an etiological aside is Gen 3.14-15:

> The LORD God said to the serpent,
>   "Because you have done this,
>   cursed are you among all animals
>   and among all wild creatures;
>   upon your belly you shall go,
>   and dust you shall eat
>   all the days of your life.
>   I will put enmity between you and the woman,
>   and between your offspring and hers;
>   he will strike your head,
>   and you will strike his heel."

In this text it is explained why the snake crawls on its belly. Also, man's habit of killing snakes instantly and violently is given legitimization. An anthropological approach treats this passage as an etiology in which both the supremacy of man over snakes as well as the power of venomous snakes to kill is expressed.

Another example of an etiological aside is Gen 3.16:

> To the woman he said,
> "I will greatly increase your pangs in childbearing;
>   in pain you shall bring forth children,
> yet your desire shall be for your husband,
>   and he shall rule over you."

In this verse an explanation is given for the fact that women suffer great pains during childbirth. This natural process of life is presented as a punishment. The supremacy of men over women is given a legitimization in this etiology. This social fact is seen as another punishment for women.

One final example of an etiological aside is Gen 3.19, where God says to Adam:

> By the sweat of your face
>   you shall eat bread
> until you return to the ground,
>   for out of it you were taken;
> you are dust,
>   and to dust you shall return.

The burdens and hardships of life are finally explained by the words of this etiology. God cursed the earth and man must work hard to get food. Life is a struggle for survival and the final destiny of man is the earth. Death is his fate.

Theological Interpretations

The traditional theological interpretations, beginning with the New Testament, have used the mythological themes and motifs as well as the etiological asides of the Garden of Eden narrative as building stones for a more profound theological message. The snake has been identified as the supernatural power of evil and the great adversary of the Creator. The mythological foolishness of the woman, who believed the snake and took fruit from the wrong tree, has been interpreted as rebellion against God, as willful disobedience. The eating of the forbidden fruit has been given a more spiritual meaning.

Scripture teaches that human beings have both emancipated and alienated themselves from the Creator. This is the essence of the historical drama of humans. In addition, the etiology of the serpent, specifically the enmity between the descendants of the snake and the human race, has been

given specific theological interpretations. The crushing of the head of the snake is interpreted by some scholars as a prophecy of a Messianic victory over the power of evil. This relates obviously to a later interpretation of the original etiological aside.

The Garden of Eden narrative contains two messages. The first one is an anti-pagan message, a contradiction of what people generally believed in the Ancient Near East about procreation, namely the belief that gods were the agents responsible for procreation. The Genesis narrative says that humans are the active agents responsible for procreation, even though it involves hardship and pain.

The second message relates to a primordial drama about the fall of human beings. Man was living with God in a garden, but alienated himself from the Creator by eating from the forbidden tree.

The Garden of Eden narrative has a clear mythological background. The mythological layer of the narrative is reflected in specific mythological language. This language mirrors fundamental thought patterns of Ancient Near Eastern religion: the polytheistic and the magical.

Translators of an ancient text such as the narrative of the Garden of Eden are sometimes tempted to base their translation unduly on the theological interpretations of the text and not on the text itself. An anthropological reading of the text can help translators become aware of the pitfalls that can lead them into a mistranslation of the original text.

Chapter 11

The Psychology of the Biblical Author

I have not dealt with the psychological factor in any specific manner so far. I have referred to value systems and social structures of ancient societies, but I have yet to focus on the personalities of the ancient narrators and writers. Ancient texts are products of ancient minds. This implies that we have to take the psychological aspect into account as we analyze the cultural context of the Bible. This valuable factor will be discussed in this chapter.

What kind of person was the ancient writer? How did he perceive life? How did his mind work? All these questions are of utmost importance if we want to read back into the mind of the Biblical author. Ancient personalities must have been different from the personalities of our time. By saying this, I am in danger of creating a dichotomy: we versus them. I am assuming that we now think differently than they did, we feel differently than they did, and we act differently from them. However, this dichotomy is a fallacy. There cannot be a dichotomy; we think and feel much the same as our early ancestors, and we have much more in common with them than we realize. The apparent differences we perceive make us blind to the similarities, and we tend to magnify the differences to the extent that we lose sight of the psychic unity that all members of humanity share with one another.

Anthropologists have written extensively on the differences between "primitive" personality and "modern" personality. They have created a dichotomy between the personalities of non-Western societies and those of modern societies, although it should be noted that in more recent literature, the fact that a continuum exists and that thinking in terms of a dichotomy is misleading has been stressed.

Lévy-Bruhl and Lévi-Strauss

The French philosopher and ethnologist, Lucien Lévy-Bruhl (1855-1939), was the first scholar to write extensively on a subject he termed "primitive mentality." He characterized the primitive mentality as prelogical and mystical. Lévy-Bruhl believed that primitive people were not capable of logical thought, as they were still in the prelogical phase of human evolution. In his view primitive people believe that all beings and objects

103

have a soul and that there are mystic relations between all animated entities. In the nineteenth century, the term animism was a common denominator for all the non-Western traditional religions. Thus, the qualification "primitive," attributed to non-Western people, was widely used. In the eyes of Lévy-Bruhl and his contemporaries, animism, which is the belief that everything has a soul (*anima* in Latin), was a source of constant error of judgment in the so-called primitive societies. The primitive man and woman ascribe cause-effect relationships to completely unrelated events. In his *Les Fonctions Mentales dans les Sociétés Inférieures* (1910), Lévy-Bruhl quotes the story of a missionary in New Guinea. The natives of New Guinea attributed the cause of an epidemic to the sheep of the missionary. The sheep were killed but the illness did not disappear. After some time it was decided that the missionary's two goats were the cause of the epidemic. Finally, it was concluded that the great portrait of Queen Victoria, which hung in the missionary's dining room, was the true cause of the illness (Lévy-Bruhl 1910:71).

This example illustrates that such causal attribution in non-Western societies can be quite unusual for Western people, but the conclusion that the primitive people are not capable of logical thought cannot be sustained. I should add here that even in modern societies one is able to observe erroneous, arbitrary, and irrational causal attribution.

In order to specify more adequately the differences between ancient and primitive thought on the one hand and modern thought on the other, we have to bring in the role of factual knowledge or, more precisely, scientific data into the cognitive process. The history of mankind shows a steady growth of knowledge. In certain periods this evolution accelerated, as was the case in the last three centuries. In certain periods growth was slower, but nevertheless the history of mankind is progressive.

The amount of objective knowledge available in a given community has a particular effect on the cognitive process of the members of that community. It domesticates thoughts and directs cause-effect attribution. We therefore can say that ancient and primitive thought is less domesticated than modern Western thought since it is less influenced by objective knowledge. However, we should not label ancient thought as pre-scientific. If we do so, we fall back into a dichotomy: modern people think scientifically and ancient people did not. We must realize that ancient people were able to think scientifically. If we think about the scientific discoveries of the Neolithic period, such as the discovery of the wheel, the wagon, the boat, weaving, pottery, and the domestication of plants and animals, we can only conclude that ancient people used scientific methods which were very similar to the ones of modern science. They were result-oriented, based their technology on factual knowledge of the world, and used empirical inductive methods of research. It is unthinkable that all major innovations of the Neolithic period were discovered accidentally; they were the fruits of scientific thought.

Lévi-Strauss gives many examples of the science of contemporary non-Western peoples in his book, *La Pensée Sauvage* (1962). Indian tribes in the forests of South America have acquired an enormous knowledge of plants

and are able to use this knowledge to cure diseases. Their medical technology is based on factual, objective knowledge of nature and their therapies on empirical research.

Lévi-Strauss has introduced a very helpful set of metaphors to refer to the differences in modes of thoughts of modern and ancient peoples. These metaphors are the *bricoleur* and the engineer. He compares the mind of the so-called primitive man with the mind of a *bricoleur*. This French word is difficult to translate into English. A *bricoleur* is someone who fixes all kind of things without being a professional carpenter or mechanic. He has his materials and tools, but he lacks the overall technical know-how. He pragmatically tries out what fits and what works, and uses what he has in his toolbox, but he does not work systematically and does not implement a preconceived plan. He does not design his instruments, but he uses what he has in his toolbox. He does not work from a design as the engineer does who applies systematic knowledge and designs the instruments he needs. The *bricoleur* is more imaginative and perceptive while the engineer is more cognitive.

Ancient man can be seen as a *bricoleur*. He did not possess an overall systematic factual knowledge of the world. He used what he had in his toolbox. He made use of the factual knowledge he had acquired, but he also used his imagination to create missing links. His thought was logical and discursive on the one hand, but also mystical and magic on the other. He applied both factual knowledge and magical knowledge.

The Growth of Consciousness

The history of humankind can be described as an evolution of consciousness. The evolutionary concept implies that early man was less conscious than modern man is. The perspective of a growing consciousness opens yet another avenue for our exploration of the personality of the ancient Biblical author. The conclusion that the ancient author was a less conscious person than a modern personality seems obvious but at the same time rather vague.

The psychologist, Julian Jaynes, wrote a thought-provoking book on the origin and growth of human consciousness. In his book, *The Origin of Consciousness in the Breakdown of the Bicameral Brain* (1977), he points out three distinctive periods in the evolution of human consciousness:

1. The period before 3000 B.C. In this period human behavior was directed by instincts and behavioral automatisms. People had a very shallow awareness of the self and the world around.
2. The period of 3000-1000 B.C. In this period during which human culture saw a rapid development, the human brain underwent significant change. It broke down into two hemispheres, the left and the right. The right hemisphere became the location where the cognitive processes took place in the neurological sense of the word. The language center and the executive functions, which stimulate and trigger actions, are

all located in the left hemisphere. The results of the cognitive processes in the right hemisphere have to be transferred neurologically through a neurological bridge to the left side where they can be transformed into language and action. This neurological bridge developed very slowly and initially was quite inadequate for rapid and efficient transfers during this particular period of human evolution. According to Jaynes, the human being of that period had a slightly split personality. The results of the cognitive processes were not recognized as decisions of the self but as voices from gods and spirits. The human being experienced life more as a puppet than as a self-regulating person.

3. The period from 1000 B.C. until our time. In this period the split between the two hemispheres was being bridged well. The brain developed a central control unit, which integrated the personality more and more. The results of the cognitive processes were gradually recognized as decisions of the self and no longer as voices from outside the person. The development of the central control unit and the corresponding awareness of the self was a gradual process that started to develop after 1000 B.C.

Jaynes mentions the prophets of ancient Israel as examples of people with two hemispheres that were not yet well connected. The prophets saw visions and heard voices. This was coming entirely from the right hemisphere and was interpreted as coming from outside, as coming from God. Jaynes traces a growing integration of the mind and an emerging concept of the self in the Biblical writings. The decline of prophecy in early Judaism is to be related to physical changes in the people's brains. A new type of prophet emerged. These prophets had a more integrated mind and a more developed self. They interpreted Scripture to reveal the will of the LORD, and did not rely on visions and voices in the same way as the ancient prophets. Cognitive processes in the interpretation and application of texts replaced hallucination.

At this point I cannot fully evaluate which part of Jaynes's theory is speculation and which is based on the hard facts of neurological research. It is obvious that the brains of people show modifications, and those people that suffer from serious schizophrenic symptoms have the particular brain deficiency Jaynes refers to. They hear voices all the time and feel that outer forces control them. It is also widely accepted that the human brain developed over the centuries along the lines indicated by Jaynes, but it also obvious that we do not have a consistent body of data covering the entire evolutionary process of the development of the human brain. My conclusion is that Jaynes's contribution to the understanding of the growth of consciousness provides us with a relevant model for our study of the differences between the personalities of ancient people and modern people. It is, however, difficult to identify hard data from his research.

Collectivist and Individualistic Types of Personalities

The British Old Testament scholar, H. Wheeler Robinson (1872-1945), made a number of helpful observations about the personality of the ancient Israelite author in his book, *The Religious Ideas of the Old Testament*, first published in 1913 (1956). He is noted for observing that ancient Israelite religion was a Semitic animism. He saw ancient Israelite religion in much the same way as Lévy-Bruhl regarded the so-called primitive society of the anthropologists. Ancient Israelites believed that everything had a soul, an immaterial component. They believed that the human being had a breath-soul (*ruach* in Hebrew) and a blood-soul (*nephesh* in Hebrew) and that these souls could leave the body during sleep and at the time of death. The human being was not seen as a bound entity, but as an open area that could be invaded by spirits and by the Spirit of the LORD at any time. Sickness was therefore normally attributed to invading spirits. The concept of an open house, which is actually a very universal representation of the human person, was a crucial notion for the understanding of ancient man.

Robinson also introduced the term "corporate personality." He observed that in the Old Testament the modern individualistic concept of the personality is absent. A person was a member of his or her family, and this implied that he or she was not only accountable for his or her own deeds but also for the deeds of other family members. This can be seen in the story of Achan in Josh 7. During the conquest led by Joshua, Achan had taken some treasures from the spoil of the city of Ai, which was devoted to the LORD. He was not killed as an individual who was the guilty person, but his whole family, including innocent children, was stoned to death and burned. Ancient Israelites had a collectivist concept of the human being. It is relevant for our understanding of the ancient Biblical author to explore the features of this concept in more detail.

The collectivist understanding of personality was widespread; it functions even in our time on a large scale. The social psychologist, Harry C. Triandis, assumes that in our time seventy percent of the world's population has remained collectivist while only thirty percent is individualistic (1990:48). An individualistic personality can be defined as follows: a bound, integrated, and self-regulating entity.

The modern personality inherent in the people of North America and Western Europe fits in the individualistic category. These modern men and women see their lives as a result of their achievements, they feel ultimately responsible for their thoughts and deeds, and they have the feeling that they own their lives. Ancient people did not have the feeling that their lives were the outcome of their own achievements. They felt very much a product of the work of their ancestors, parents, and family members. They only felt a limited responsibility for their own thoughts and deeds since they believed they were controlled to a large extent by other human beings and supernatural forces. They did not feel that they owned their lives. They had a different perception of their lives than modern people have.

Three Features of the Collectivist Type of Personality

The three main features of the collectivist concept of personality are dependency, embeddedness in social groups, and obligation to social groups. Initially, there is the feeling of dependency. Ancient man did not believe that he was the architect of his own life. He strongly felt a product of the process of enculturation and socialization that he had undergone as a child. He also felt that supernatural forces influenced his entire life and that there was very limited room for personal choices. His destiny, fate, and luck were determined from the day of his birth, and his entire life was in the hands of forces beyond his own control.

Second, he felt embedded in in-groups, such as his family, social classes, and political groups. It is important to realize that embeddedness is not identical to membership. Ancient persons felt psychologically embedded in their kinship group and other groups. They experienced their lives as rooted in their in-groups in such a manner that they perceived their existence as fully integrated in their groups. They did not perceive themselves as independent individuals in their own right. Ancient man felt he was a son of so and so; for example, a man from the clan of Caleb, a free man of the tribe of Benjamin, an Israelite and not a Philistine. In particular, kinship groups and gender determined the basic structures of the identity of a person. As a professional, he belonged to a certain class, be it the class of blacksmiths, soldiers, or flute players. This allegiance further determined his behavior and identity.

Third, the collectivist person regards life primarily as an obligation to the groups he is imbedded in. In honor-oriented societies, a person has no other choice than to follow the honor codes of his group. A member of a noble family has to defend the position of his family in contests at all costs. He does not have the freedom to back out of a situation where the honor of the family is at stake. A soldier must be courageous, and is not allowed to show fear of death. He has to respect the code of his group.

The collectivist personality sees success in life in terms of being able to fulfil the obligations he has towards the in-groups he belongs to. He does not evaluate life in terms of personal fulfilment and achievement. He does not want to be different, to be someone special; he aspires to be alike, to conform to the codes of the groups he belongs to.

Paul as an Example of a Collectivist Personality

Bruce J. Malina and Jerome H. Neyrey present a portrait of Paul as a collectivist personality in their book, *Portraits of Paul: An Archaeology of Ancient Personality* (1996). They rightly observe that Paul makes many references to himself in his writings, and as such he is unique among the Biblical authors, but that he never refers to specific distinctive characteristics of his individual psyche. He frequently declares his dependency. He refers often to his own embeddedness and almost constantly speaks about his obligations. Paul often refers to his ultimate dependency. All what he

does is what Christ does in him. All he has in terms of knowledge and insight he has received from a source outside himself.

Paul sees his whole life in terms of dependency and embeddedness. He refers to himself as "a Hebrew born of Hebrews" (Php 3.5), a descendant of Abraham (2 Cor 11.22), and a Judean man, born in the city of Tarsus, educated by the Pharisees in Jerusalem (Acts 22.3). Above all, he presents himself as a slave and servant of God and Jesus Christ. He sees himself as one whom Christ directly called through visions to be an apostle to Jews and Gentiles. His conversion on the road to Damascus changed his outlook entirely. Christ appeared to him in a vision. The change of direction in his life was not a personal choice, an achievement, or a change growing from a developing insight; it was a sudden intervention of Christ (Acts 9).

Paul identified himself with the Old Testament prophets who also were directly called and commissioned by God through visions to speak the word of God. The prophets were not left with a choice; they felt utterly obliged to communicate the divine revelation they received for the people. Paul also felt obliged to preach the gospel of Jesus Christ, first to the Jews and then to the Gentiles (Rom 9–11).

The personality of Paul is an example of a collectivist person who sees his life as the plan and work of others. For Paul the others were his ancestors, teachers, and, above all, God and Jesus Christ.

Concluding Remarks

The subject matter of this particular chapter has led me to generalizations and simplifications that need careful interpretation. We have noticed that there is very little psychology in Biblical writing. Also, we have little available information about the authors themselves. We must even admit that the very concept of authorship is not always clear-cut, particularly with regard to the Old Testament writings. Should we regard the Yahwist, who is the source of most of the Genesis narratives, as an author, or should we see him more as a narrator whose narration was collected and heavily edited by others? When we speak about the psychology of the Biblical author, we need to distinguish between different authors from different periods in history; for example, the Yahwist (900 B.C.) and Paul (50 A.D.). We tend to ignore the apparent differences, and so we position them both under the denominator of Biblical author in order to juxtapose them with the modern personality. Despite the shortcomings of this methodology, it helps to focus on important nuances. I would like to summarize my findings along these lines and offer a chart on the next page that helps to map the basic differences between the ancient personality and the modern one. However, we should keep in mind that in many categories we cannot speak of a dichotomy, but rather of a modification of degree.

Modifications in Cognitive Functions

Ancient Personality	Modern Personality
Wild thinking	Domesticated thinking
Mystical thought patterns	Mechanical, scientific thinking
Mythological thought (see Chapter 9)	Evolutionary, historical thinking
Ritual thought (see Chapter 8)	Psychological thought
Concrete thinking	Abstract thinking
Bricolage	Engineering
Perceptive and imaginative thinking	Rational thinking

Modifications related to Social Categories

Ancient Personality	Modern Personality
Collectivist	Individualistic
High sense of dependency	Sense of independence
Conformation to social groups	Expression of personal characteristics
Obligation	Freedom to choose

Modifications related to the Concept of the Self

Ancient Personality	Modern Personality
Less bounded	Bounded
Less integrated	Integrated
Less self-regulating	More self-regulating

Epilogue

The Biblical text originated in the Ancient Near East. This implies that it can only be given a meaningful interpretation within the cultural context of the Ancient Near East. In this book I have presented a number of anthropological approaches that enable a reader to come closer to the realities of the world behind the Biblical account. Given the fact that it is impossible to give a complete description of the cultural context of the Bible, I have introduced several models from anthropology and sociology that can be used to create a general picture of the cultural context.

The anthropological model of ancient religion is extremely relevant for a contextual interpretation of the Bible. The fact that the ancient peoples lived in a world dominated by gods should be held at the forefront of our minds. Their world-view was polytheistic and magical. Ancestor worship was also an important element of their religion. Ancient peoples were always in need of knowledge about the causes of fortune and misfortune; divination was a necessity of life. Their knowledge of natural causes for disaster was limited. They had not yet secularized the world. People in the Ancient Near East felt surrounded by hostile forces and powers. Their view of the world was dominated by the magical and not by the secular or scientific, as is the case with modern people. We must realize that there is a wide gap between the symbolic universe of the Biblical author and that of the modern reader.

The apocalyptic universe is a key symbolic structure for a contextual interpretation of the writings of the New Testament. It modifies the basic structures of the model of Ancient Near Eastern religion.

The Biblical text reflects important breakthroughs in the cultural evolution of human beings. Biblical authors present new elements of thought. These new ideas are new in the cultural context of the Ancient Near East, yet they may not be altogether new for a modern reader. These cultural innovations are not always made explicit. Often they are expressed poetically, and at times they are framed as mythological critique that sometimes is only alluded to. This means that a modern reader must be very alert and read between the lines for what is behind the words of the text. In the first chapter of the Bible, we are presented with a wide spectrum of new ideas. I will highlight two interesting cases of new ideas expressed in the text.

In the first chapter of the book of Genesis, we read:

> Then God said, "Let the earth put forth vegetation: plants yielding seed, and fruit trees of every kind on earth that bear fruit with the seed in it." And it was so. The earth brought forth vegetation: plants yielding seed of every kind, and trees of every kind bearing fruit with the seed in it. And God saw that is was good (Gen 1.11-12)

The message that every plant and tree produces seed seems to be of no importance for a modern reader. He knows perfectly well how plants and trees multiply, having the benefit of factual knowledge of the natural process of growth from biological science. Ancient people did not have this knowledge; they believed that certain vegetation gods created new plants and trees in springtime and that the people had to enhance the process of growth by sacrifices and other ritual actions. The text of Genesis contains therefore an important message for the reader. Translators of the Bible who deem the explicit mentioning of seed as unimportant and redundant may decide to streamline the text by omitting the phrases, "yielding seed" and "bearing fruit with the seed in it." Regrettably, an important element of the message of the original text is then lost in translation.

In the first chapter of Genesis, we also read:

> Then God said, "Let us make humankind in our image, according to our likeness; and let them have dominion over the fish of the sea, and over the birds of the air, and over the cattle, and over all the wild animals of the earth, and over every creeping thing that creeps upon the earth."
> So God created humankind in his image,
> in the image of God he created them;
> male and female he created them (Gen 1.26-27).

This text does not simply recount the moment of the creation of man. It contains a very powerful message about the very nature and destiny of man. Man is created in the likeness of the Creator; he bears his image. In other words he is his representative on earth. Furthermore, he is given dominion over all the creatures of the universe. A modern reader may not be surprised, but an ancient hearer or reader receives an intriguing message. In the Ancient Near East, people believed that kings were created in the likeness of the gods. Kings were seen as representatives of the gods among the ordinary people. Common people were creatures of a lower quality, so to speak. They were not given dominion over all the creatures of the universe; only kings could have these powers. A good translation of these verses from Genesis must open up the hidden message for modern readers.

Again, it must be reiterated that Biblical translation and interpretation should be contextual. The Bible has a long history of being interpreted out of context. Many translations suffer from a lack of contextual consistency. This holds true for a number of modern translations.

The Biblical text is part of ancient culture. An anthropological approach to the Bible looks for ways to come closer to the symbolic systems the text refers to. It is useful to employ different reading scenarios as windows on the symbolic world behind the Biblical text. The most powerful reading scenario is the anthropological model of ancient religion. Others, such as the social value complex, the ritual structure, and myth, prove to be equally helpful.

Anthropological approaches to the Bible aim at bridging the gap between the symbolic universe of the Biblical writer and that of the modern reader. It is a task that can never be completely fulfilled. The cultural identity of the Biblical author differed from the modern personality. Also, his cognitive functions were different. However, it is my conviction that the modern reader can understand the psychological and symbolic world of ancient man. I also believe that more ground should and can be covered in this area, considering that valuable research into the cultural world of the Ancient Near East progresses. There is growth in the insight that the cultural context is paramount to conveying the intended message of the Biblical text.

Bibliography

Alter, Robert, and Frank Kermode, editors. 1987. *The Literary Guide to the Bible*. Cambridge, Massachusetts: Harvard University Press.

van Baal, Jan. 1981. *Man's Quest for Partnership: The Anthropological Foundations of Ethics and Religion*. Assen: Van Gorcum.

van Baal, Jan, and W. E. A. van Beek. 2nd revised edition, 1985. *Symbols for Communication: An Introduction to the Anthropological Study of Religion*. Assen: Van Gorcum.

Beier, Ulli, editor. 1966. *The Origin of Life and Death: African Creation Myths*. London: Heineman.

Bell, Catherine M. 1992. *Ritual Theory, Ritual Practice*. New York: Oxford University Press.

Black, Jeremy A.; Anthony Green; and Tessa Rickards. 1992. *Gods, Demons, and Symbols of Ancient Mesopotamia: An Illustrated Dictionary*. London: British Museum Press.

Brett, Mark G. 2000. *Genesis: Procreation and the Politics of Identity*. London and New York: Routledge.

Brichto, Herbert Chanan. 1998. *The Names of God: Poetic Readings in Biblical Beginnings*. New York: Oxford University Press.

Burkert, Walter. 1996. *Creation of the Sacred: Tracks of Biology in Early Religions*. Cambridge, Massachusetts: Harvard University Press.

Burkert, Walter; René Girard; and Jonathan Z. Smith. 1987. *Violent Origins: Ritual Killing and Cultural Formation*. Edited by Robert G. Hamerton-Kelly. Stanford: Stanford University Press.

Coupe, Laurence. 1997. *Myth*. London and New York: Routledge.

Cryer, Frederick H. 1994. *Divination in Ancient Israel and Its Near Eastern Environment: A Socio-Historical Investigation* (Journal for the Study of the Old Testament Supplement Series, 142). Sheffield: JSOT Press.

115

Curvers, Hans H. 1992. *Dorpen en Steden van Klei: Van Boer tot Burger in Mesopotamië*. Amsterdam: Amsterdam University Press.

Davies, Philip. R. 1992. *In Search of "Ancient Israel"* (Journal for the Study of the Old Testament Supplement Series, 148). Sheffield: JSOT Press.

Davies, Philip R., and David J. A. Clines, editors. 1998. *The World of Genesis: Persons, Places, Perspectives* (Journal for the Study of the Old Testament Supplement Series, 257). Sheffield: Sheffield Academic Press.

Douglas, Mary. 1966. *Purity and Danger: An Analysis of the Concepts of Pollution and Taboo*. London: Routledge and Kegan Paul.

———. 1999. *Leviticus as Literature*. Oxford and New York: Oxford University Press.

Ehrman, Bart D. 1999. *Jesus, Apocalyptic Prophet of the New Millennium*. Oxford and New York: Oxford University Press.

Frazer, James George. 1922; abridged edition, 1994. *The Golden Bough: A History of Myth and Religion*. London: Chancellor Press.

Freud, Sigmund. 1913. *Totem und Tabu: Einige Übereinstimmungen in Seelenleben der Wilden und der Neurotiker*. Leipzig: H. Heller.

Geertz, Clifford. 1983. *Local Knowledge: Further Essays in Interpretative Anthropology*. New York: Basic Books.

———. 1973, 2000. *The Interpretation of Cultures: Selected Essays*. New York: Basic Books.

van Gennep, Arnold. 1909. *Les Rites de Passage*. Paris: É. Nourry.

Ginzberg, Louis. 1992. *Legends of the Bible*. Philadelphia: Jewish Publication Society.

Girard, René; Jean-Michel Oughourlian; and Guy Lefort. 1978. *Des Choses Cachées Depuis la Fondation du Monde*. Paris: B. Grasset.

———. 1982. *Le Bouc Émissaire*. Paris: B. Grasset.

Goodison, Lucy, and Christine Morris, editors. 1998. *Ancient Goddesses: The Myths and the Evidence*. London: British Museum Press.

Goody, Jack. 1977. *The Domestication of the Savage Mind*. Cambridge, England: Cambridge University Press.

Gottwald, Norman K. 1979. *The Tribes of Yahweh: A Sociology of the Religion of Liberated Israel, 1250-1050 B.C.E.* Maryknoll, New York: Orbis Books.

Guenther, Mathias Georg. 1999. *Tricksters and Trancers: Bushman Religion and Society.* Bloomington: Indiana University Press.

Habel, Norman C. 1985. *The Book of Job* (The Old Testament Library). London: SCM Press.

Hall, Edward Twitchell. 1976. *Beyond Culture.* Garden City, New York: Anchor Press.

The Holy Bible: New Revised Standard Version. 1989. New York: Division of Christian Education of the National Council of Churches of Christ in the United States of America.

Jacobsen, Thorkild. 1976. *The Treasures of Darkness: A History of Mesopotamian Religion.* New Haven: Yale University Press.

van der Jagt, Krijn A. 1983. *De Religie van de Turkana van Kenia.* Ph.D. Dissertation, University of Utrecht.

———. 1989. *Symbolic Structures in Turkana Religion.* Assen: Van Gorcum.

———. 1994. "The Genesis Narratives in Anthropological Perspective." In *Current Trends in Scripture Translation* (United Bible Societies Bulletin, Number 170/171, pages 130-137). Reading, England: United Bible Societies.

———. 1996. "What Did Saul Eat When He Visited Samuel?" *The Bible Translator* 47:226-230.

Jaynes, Julian. 1977. *The Origin of Consciousness in the Breakdown of the Bicameral Mind.* Boston: Houghton Mifflin.

Jeffers, Ann. 1996. *Magic and Divination in Ancient Palestine and Syria.* Leiden: E. J. Brill.

Kirk, G. S. 1974. *The Nature of Greek Myths.* London: Penguin.

Kramer, Samuel Noah. 1963. *The Sumerians: Their History, Culture, and Character.* Chicago: University of Chicago Press.

Kuper, Hilda. 1952. *The Swazi.* London: International African Institute.

Leach, Edmund Ronald, and D. Alan Aycock. 1983. *Structuralist Interpretations of Biblical Myth.* Cambridge, England: Cambridge University Press.

Lévy-Bruhl, Lucien. 1910. *Les Fonctions Mentales dans les Sociétés Inférieures*. Paris: F. Alcan.

Lévi-Strauss, Claude. 1958. *Anthropologie Structurale*. Paris: Plon.

———. 1962. *La Pensée Sauvage*. Paris: Plon.

Lewis, I. M. 1971; 2nd edition, 1989. *Ecstatic Religion: A Study of Shamanism and Spirit Possession*. London and New York: Routledge.

Loretz, Oswald. 1990. *Ugarit und die Bibel: Kanaanäische Götter und Religion im Alten Testament*. Darmstadt: Wissenschaftliche Buchgesellschaft.

Malina, Bruce J., and Jerome H. Neyrey 1996. *Portraits of Paul: An Archaeology of Ancient Personality*. Louisville: Westminster John Knox Press.

Masson, O. 1950. "A propos d'un rituel Hittite pour la lustration d'une armee." *Revue de l'Histoire des Religions* 137.5-25.

Matthews, Victor Harold; Don C. Benjamin; and Claudia V. Camp. 1996. *Honor and Shame in the World of the Bible* (Semeia, 68). Atlanta: Scholars Press.

Matthews, Victor Harold, and Don C. Benjamin. 1993 *Social World of Ancient Israel, 1250-587 BCE*. Peabody, Massachusetts: Hendrikson Publishers.

Mazar, Amihay. 1990. *Archaeology of the Land of the Bible, 10,000-586 B.C.E.* New York: Doubleday.

McVann, Mark, and Bruce J. Malina, editors. 1995. *Transformations, Passages, and Processes: Ritual Approaches to Biblical Texts* (Semeia, 67). Atlanta: Scholars Press.

Meier, John P. 1991. *A Marginal Jew: Rethinking the Historical Jesus*, Volume 1 (*The Roots of the Problem and the Person*). New York: Doubleday.

———. 1994. *A Marginal Jew: Rethinking the Historical Jesus*, Volume 2 (*Mentor, Message and Miracles*). New York: Doubleday.

Miller, Patrick D.; Paul D. Hanson; and S. Dean McBride, editors. 1987. *Ancient Israelite Religion: Essays in Honor of Frank Moore Cross*. Philadelphia: Fortress Press.

Morris, Brian. 1987. *Anthropological Studies of Religion: An Introductory Text*. Cambridge, England: Cambridge University Press.

Neyrey, Jerome H., editor. 1991. *The Social World of Luke–Acts: Models for Interpretation*. Peabody, Massachusetts: Hendrickson Publishers.

Niditch, Susan. 1997. *Ancient Israelite Religion*. New York: Oxford University Press.

Noss, Philip A. 2001. "Wanto and Laaiso and the Gbaya Bible: The Trickster and His Wife in Scripture Translation." *The Bible Translator* 52:114-132.

Oppenheim, A. Leo. 1964. *Ancient Mesopotamia: Portrait of a Dead Civilization*. Chicago: University of Chicago Press.

Péristiany, Jean G., editor. 1966. *Honour and Shame: The Values of Mediterranean Society*. Chicago: University of Chicago Press.

Pritchard, James Bennett, editor. 3rd edition, 1969. *Ancient Near Eastern Texts Relating to the Old Testament*. Princeton: Princeton University Press.

Reviv, Hanoch. 1989. *The Elders of Ancient Israel: A Study of a Biblical Institution*. Jerusalem: Magnes Press.

Robinson, H. Wheeler. 1913; 2nd edition, 1956. *The Religious Ideas of the Old Testament*. Revised by L. H. Brockington. London: G. Duckworth.

Rogerson, J. W. 1978, 1984. *Anthropology and the Old Testament*. Sheffield: JSOT Press.

Sieber, Johannes. 1925. *Die Wute: Lebenshaltung, Kultur und Religiöse Weltanschauung eines Afrikanischen Volksstammes*. Berlin: Dietrich Reimer.

Snell, Daniel C. 1997. *Life in the Ancient Near East, 3100-332 B.C.E.* New Haven: Yale University Press.

Soggin, J. Alberto. 2nd edition, 1993. *An Introduction to the History of Israel and Judah*. Translated by John Bowden. Valley Forge, Pennsylvania: Trinity Press International.

Speiser, E. A. 1964; 3rd edition, 1987. *Genesis: Introduction, Translation, and Notes* (The Anchor Bible, 1). Garden City, New York: Doubleday.

Theissen, Gerd. 1977. *Soziologie der Jesusbewegung*. Munchen: Kaiser.

BIBLIOGRAPHY

van der Toorn, Karel. 1996. *Family Religion in Babylonia, Syria, and Israel: Continuity and Changes in the Forms of Religious Life*. Leiden: E. J. Brill.

Triandis, Harry Charalambos. 1990. "Cross-Cultural Studies of Individualism and Collectivism" In *Nebraska Symposium on Motivation*, pages 41-133. Edited by J. Berman. Lincoln: University of Nebraska Press.

Turner, Victor Witter. 1967. *The Forest of Symbols: Aspects of Ndembu Ritual*. Ithaca, New York: Cornell University Press.

———. 1969. *The Ritual Process: Structure and Anti-Structure*. London: Routledge and Kegan Paul.

Tubb, Jonathan N. 1998. *Peoples of the Past: Canaanites*. London: British Museum Press.

Wilson, A. N. 1992. *Jesus*. London: Sinclair-Stevenson.

Worsley, Peter. 1957; 2nd edition, 1968. *The Trumpet Shall Sound: A Study of "Cargo" Cults in Melanesia*. London: Macgibbon and Kee.

PRINTED IN THE UNITED STATES OF AMERICA

Anthropological Approaches
to the
Interpretation of the Bible